C000271056

Birds & Mammals
of Cyprus

*Although Cyprus and her people
have been torn as under.
They keep being united by the birds
flying in the same sky.*

                 G. Sfikas

George Sfikas

Birds & Mammals of Cyprus

EFSTATHIADIS GROUP S.A.

© Efstathiadis Group 2006

ISBN: 960-226-295-8

EFSTATHIADIS GROUP S.A.
88 Drakontos Str.,
104 42 Athens
tel.: ++3210 5195 800,
fax: ++3210 5195 940
e-mail: info@efgroup.gr
www.efgroup.gr
GREECE

Printed and bound in Greece

INTRODUCTION - SOME HISTORICAL NOTES

Mythology tells us that Cyprus is the island Aphrodite first dwelt on after she sprang - as her Greek name indicates - from the foam of the sea.

The first traces of human inhabitance on Cyprus originate from the 6th millenium B.C.*, at the time when the peoples of the countries bordering the East Mediterranean were, for the first time, successful in crossing the sea and establishing themselves on the various islands in that region. In fact, Crete and the Aegean islands appear to have been peopled at about that time.

In that long past age the whole of Cyprus was covered with boundless: forests in which a multitude of wild mammals and birds lived. The original human inhabitants on the island came from the opposite shores of Asia Minor and the Middle East. These settlers are known today as Eteocypriots. It was they who discovered the island's rich deposits of copper and, already from the 3rd milleniun B.C.*, turned them to good account. Fifteen hundred years later Mycenean merchants started coming from Greece and establishing themselves on the island, to be followed later in the 10th century B.C., by the Phoenicians to whom we owe the name of Cyprus, a derivation of their word for copper.

By Homeric times the hellenising of Cyprus had already gained considerable ground and the island has ever since been linguistically, historically, and culturally linked to Greece. Although later Cyprus became part first of the Assyrian Empire, then of the Egyptian, and lastly of the Persian, it never lost its Greekness.

At the time of Alexander the Great (336-323 B.C.) Cyprus became part of his vast Macedonian Empire, but with the splitting of the Empire after its founder's death it came under the Ptolemies of Egypt until 58 B.C. when it was conquered by the Romans.

In the Byzantine era the island passed into the domain of the Eastern Roman Empire, thus forming part of the Byzantine State and becoming one with it in language, culture and religion, and though frequently attacked by the Arabs it was always successful in repelling their assaults, Several centuries of Byzantine government followed before Cyprus finally succumbed, in 1191, to Richard the Lion-hearted. His ally, Guy de Luscignan King of Jerusalem, took over the ruling of the island. Thus began the period of Frankish dominion under the independent Frankish sovereignty of the de Luscignans.

In that period trade flourished enormously. Among other things the cultivation of the sugar-cane was developed in order to produce sugar for export to Europe. This crop today is completely unknown on the island.

In 1489 Cyprus passed from the Frankish rule to that of the Venetians, which rule lasted up to 1571 when the island was conquered by the Turks. The latter held the island up to 1878 when they ceded it to Britain in a private agreement as a temporary military base. In 1914 (when the First World War broke out) Britain cancelled this agreement and annexed Cyprus to the British Empire.

British Rule was at last terminated in 1960, and Cyprus declared an independent State - henceforth called the Republic of Cyprus but still remaining within the framework of the British Commonwealth. In 1974 an attempt was made by a small group of extreme-right-wingers to

* Traces from 8th millenium BC. were discovered recently.

Aphrodite's Rock, there where - according to tradition - the goddess of Beauty was born.

establish a Dictatorship that would dismiss the legitimate Government of Archbishop Macarios. The Turkish Government swiftly reacted and sent a Turkish army to invade the island under the excuse of protecting the Turkish minority there. Ever since, Cyprus has been divided into two separate regions: the larger southern sector, which continues to constitute the Republic of Cyprus and is recognised as such by the U.N. and the other international organisations, and the northern sector, unlawfully declared a Turco-Cypriot State, composed of but a small number of citizens, and recognised as an independent state by no other country save Turkey.

The boundary line dividing the Greek Cypriot State from the Turkish one runs across the central plain. Morphou and Famagusta are inside the Turkish sector, while the capital, Nicosia, is traversed by the dividing line splitting it into two.

The consequences of the Turkish invasion have not left the natural environment, in particular the fauna, unaffected. In the northern sector the sudden drop in population, caused by the expulsion of the Greek Cypriots from the region, has resulted in the desolation of the land, preeminently in the fertile and cultivated zones. In point of fact, such a condition could favour the increase of the fauna were it not that the invading troops don't have to give an account of their actions to anyone and that new settlers are constantly arriving from Turkey. But the worst are the crowd of adventurers who according to available information are systematically annihilating the rare island birds, such as the Cypriot partridge (Alectoris chukarcypriotes) and the Francolin (Francolinus francolinus).

Sunset near the town Poli Chrisokhus. The sun is sinking behind Akamas Point.

Unfortunately, in the southern also sector of Cyprus the consequences of the encroachment on the natural environment can be clearly discerned. One has but to consider what the abrupt increase in population, caused by the influx of the Cypriot refugees, has resulted in: - a rapid development of urban centres which, in turn, has turned large tracts of land, both inland and coastal, into building areas. Formerly, these regions maintained an interesting variety of flora and fauna.

In addition, some of the most beautiful forests were burnt at the time of the invasion, principally those in the Paphos district. Fortunately, however, this mischief has been repaired by a swift and successful afforestation campaign instituted by the Forestry Department of the competent Ministry of the Cypriot Republic.

But there are other reasons also for the degradation of the natural environment. For instance, in the Greek Cypriot sector an inordinate growth in the number of tourists is to be observed, thus leading to the coast being rapidly turned into tourist centres with their vast hotel complexes. Another deplorable feature is the constant increase in the number of sportsmen, or 'hunters' as they are called there, as well as a relative increase in poaching.

Naturally, at the present time the main preoccupation of the Cypriot Government is the problem of resettling the refugees on the one hand, and the efforts to make Cyprus once again the single independent state it was before 1974 on the other. Regarding the natural environment, while it is adequately protected in the large state-owned forests of the Troodos massif, on the contrary the pressures and threats to it in the littoral zone are great, as will be seen further on.

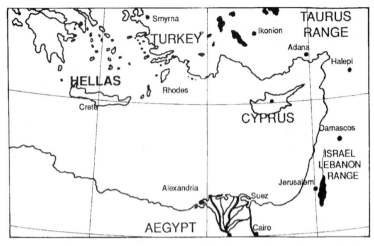

Lying in the East Mediterranean and surrounded by three continents, Cyprus has always been a crossroads where we come upon elements of Asian, European and African fauna.

GEOGRAPHICAL DATA

Cyprus is the third largest Mediterranean island after Sicily and Sardinia. It has an area of 9,250 square kilometres. The maximum length is 226 kms while its greatest width is 96 kms. The northern coastline lies more or less parallel to that of Turkey, a distance of only 72 kms separating Cape Acrotiri from the Turkish shores.

The greater part of the eastern coastline is between 160-180 kms distant from Syria; however, the Cape St. Andreas is only 105 kms away. The Lebanon, too, is very close, its capital Beirut just 175 kms distant from Cape Greco towards the south-east.

The island is dominated by two mountain ranges lying parallel to each other, in a general west-east direction, and separated by an extensive plain.

To the north the Pentadhactylos (Five-Fingered) Range - also known as the Kyrenia Range - forms a continuous wall that isolates the interior from the sea. It starts from Kornos Peak in the west near Cape Kormakitis and ends as a range of hills along the Karpassia Peninsula. The highest points of the Pentadhactylos Range are: Kyparissovouno (1024 m) and Buffavento (955 m). There are, however, several more peaks over 700 m in height, such as: Kornos (946m), Trypa Vouno or Alonagra (935 m), Yaila (935 m), Olympos (740 m), Prophitis Elias (858 m), Palia Vryssi (819 m), Mount Sinai or Kantara (824 m) and, lastly, the Pentadhactylos Peak (740 m) whose characteristic five points make it conspicuous and eye-catching from afar, thus justly bestowing its name on the whole range.

In the southern half of Cyprus the Troodos Range extends with peaks almost double the height of those of the Pentadhactylos range. The highest summit is Khionistra or Olympos (1961 m). Other noteworthy peaks are: Papoutsa (1554 m), Kionia or Makheras (1423 m), Madhari or Adelphi (1612 m), Tripylos (1362 m), Zacharou (1212 m), North Shoulder (1709 m), Kalliphon (1158 m), Stavropefkos (1234 m) and several more of lesser height.

The section of the island situated between the two ranges is flatter towards the eastern end of the island, while at the opposite western end there is a range of hills which, at certain points (Xeri, Aghia Marina), rises to a height of over 300 m.

There is a comparatively narrow lowland zone in the south of Cyprus lying between the sea and the Troodos Range, while small lowland tracks can be found also in the long, narrow Karpassia Peninsula at the N.E. end of the island.

The short mountain torrents which descend mainly from the Troodos Range can hardly be styled rivers, since most of them dry up in the summer. The longest river is the Pedhiaios (95 kms. long) which flows across the central plain down into Famagusta Bay. There also used to be interesting fresh-water marshes at Fasouri and Limasol. Unfortunately they have now been drained.

Finally, mention must be made of the two salt lakes found in Larnaca and Limasol for they are of immense importance to the migratory birds.

GEOLOGY

The greater part of the island's coastline is stony and rocky, there are, however, a number of sandy beaches scattered all along the whole littoral zone, while in the regions of Famagusta and Karpassia there are dunes and sandy tracts.

The Pentadhactylos Range, the older of the two mountain massifs, was formed at the time of the Alpine orogenesis and consists of Permian, Carboniferous and Cretaceous limestone interrupted by basaltic layers. On the lower slopes one comes across Miocene marl, sandstone, and conglomerates. There is a scarcity of water in the area; however, some important springs are to be found near the villages of Lapithos and Caravas that irrigate endless groves of citrus fruit.

On the contrary the Troodos Range is of volcanic origin, composed of serpentine, gabbro, diabase and pillow-lava. It also originated later, and its rocky crust (lithosphere) is rich in minerals such as: amianthus, chromite, iron pyrites and copper pyrites whence copper is obtained and which has endowed the island with wealth and power ever since antiquity.

The central plain is formed chiefly of clay, marl, and testaceous limestone, while in the areas around the Troodos we frequently come across chalk limestone and gypsum.

The Akamas Peninsula at the west end of Cyprus is of particular geological interest on account of the great diversity of its rocks and the resulting variety of vegetation.

THE EMERGENCE OF CYPRUS

Approximately 70 million years ago, the entire area of the Mediterranean, where present day

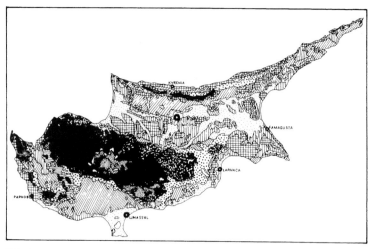

Alluvium		Pillow-Lavas und Basal Group
Terrace Deposits		Diabase
Nicosia - Athalassa Formations		Plagiogranite
Kalavasos, Koronia, Pakhna, Kythrea Formations		Gabbro
Terra. Lefkara, Ardana - Kalogrea und Lapithos Formations		Pyroxenite, Dunite, Wehrlite
Moni, Kannaviou and Perapedi Formations		Harzburgite, Serpentinite
Hilarion, Sykhari, Dhikomo and Kantara Formations.		Serpentinite (Mamonia Complex)
Mamonia Complex		

A geological map of Cyprus where one can clearly see both the volcanic origin of the Troodos Range and the great variety of rocks in the Akamas Peninsula.

Cyprus lies, was covered by the sea. The level of the sea began to rise during this period as a result of the leightened movement of the ocean's floor and the earth's outer crust. This heightened movement resulted in the immersion of the African continental plate below the Euroasian plate.

It is an established fact that Africa is slowly shifting towards the north and creating pressure on southern Europe and western Asia. The direct consequence of this movement is the numerous volcanoes which are found in the southern Aegean, on northern Crete as well as on Milos, Santorini, Nyssyros and many other islands.

This was not the case on Cyprus, where volcanoes did not appear. Here, a very slow progression of ascent began which was intensified by the fact that the upper rock formations of the earth's crust were in direct contact with the water which had been created by the overlap of the two continental plates. As a result, these petrifications where acted upon and

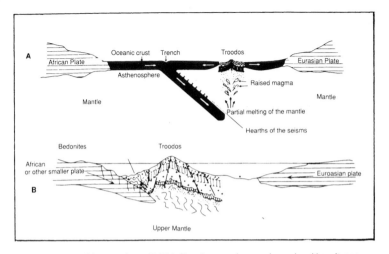

A reconstruction of the way the ophiolithic Troodos complex was formed and how it rose. (Great Cypriote Encyclopedia, 1986).

altered by absorption, and so their actual weight decreased whili their size increased.

By this process, a large underwater mountain was formed which repuired 50 million years to actually emerge from the sea. Thus 20 million years ago, on the site where present day Cyprus lies, a small and narrow island appeared which slowly grew in size. This small island was the present day mountain range of Troodous. 5 million years later (approximately 15 million years ago) another island emerges north of the first island. This island was the precursor of the present day mountain range of Ciryneias or Pentadaktilou and came into existance after a tectonic earthquake, whose movements occured along a north-south axis, and which caused a fold in the ocean's floor.

THE COLONIZATION OF PLANTS AND ANIMALS

The two islands remained isolated from each other as well as from neighbouring Western Asia for 8.5 million years. As they had never come into physical contact with the neighbouring lands, their colonization of plants and wild life was very difficult, and indeed for some species, impossible. Plants, such as sea irises (Pancratium maritimum) and pines (Pinus pinea) whose seeds are carried on the ocean waves quickly took root on the islands' shores. Ohter plants, more notibly the different Compositae species, whose seeds are carried by the winds, quickly grew in the interior areas of the island. Finally, those seeds which are carried by birds via their peptic system also evolved on the two islands, which

11

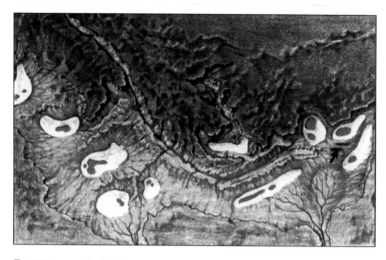

The drying up of the Mediterranean 6,5 million years ago resulted in the two islands that existed then where Cyprus is now; they were joined so closely together as well as with the adjacent continents that many species of plants and animals were able to emigrate there.

offered the migrating birds a place to rest. Several of the birds found the new land ideal places to build their nests and to hatch their offsprings. It is unlikely however that during this time Cyprus received mammals, reptiles or snails.

Ironically, 6.5 million years ago the sea, which was an obstacle in that it occurance. The continual pressure of Africa on Europe resulted in the complete closure of the Straits of Gibraltar and the isolation of the Mediterranean sea frome the Atlantic Ocean. Rivers such as the Rhone, the Nile and other smaller rivers were incapable of receiving the vast amount of water which was pushed out and lost frome the Mediterranean as a result of the closure.

Thus, after a short period of time, the Mediterranean was transformed int a deep, warm and dry valley, and only at its lowest levels were there large salt water lakes. in this way, essential bridges were formed which allowed multifarious plants and animals from the neighbouring mainlands to cross over to the Cypriot island, a fact which, if unknown, would have made their existance on the islands unfeasable.

5.3 million years ago the Atlantic ocean once again broke the Straits of Gibraltar and this resulted in a great flood which poured down into the Mediterranean. It is estimated that the waterfall created had a height of 3000 meters, a force five times greater than that of Niagara Falls and 40 cubic miles of water poured into the Mediterranean basin each day. Thus in one century the Mediterranean filled once again and all the animals and plants which had migrated to the two Cypriot islands were islated frome their co-species in Asia and Africa.

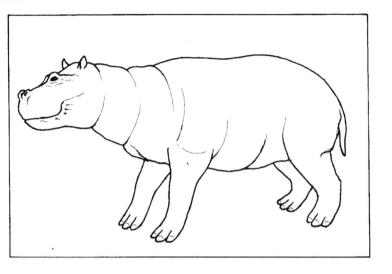

The pygmy Cyprus hippopotamus (Hippopotamus fanurius). The reconstruction was made by the author, based on a photograph of the skeleton.

Many of these species have remained unaltered frome this period, such as the Alnus orientalis, a tree which grows in river beds; the Asphodeline brevicaulis; the Campanula peregrina and the Fritillaria persica which are plants founds also in Western Asia. Animals such as the Fox and the Hare which are common to the surrounding lands have also remained as they were. Others, such as large carniverous animals must have disappeared soon after their arrival because their natural habitat became restricted. On the other hand, several species not only survived but over the course of time evolved to adapt to their new surroundings and deviated in appearance from their former kindred species in Africa and Asia. With respect to plants we can cite over one hundred such species which developed into indigenous types. Several such examples are Quercus alnifolia which originally derived from the Euroasian species. Q. ilex; the Tulipa cypria which is closely related to the Turkish. T. agenesis; the Cedrus libanii-brevilolia, a close relation to the Cedar tree of Lebanon; the Euphorbia veneris which is closely related to the Euroasian E. rigida and many more.

As for the animals, we can recall many types such as the Acomys nesiotes, a close relative to the African A. cahirinus; the Crocidura cypria, a close relative to the euroasian C. russula; and the Agrinio (Cypriot wild sheep) which is related to the species Ovis musimon. Similar changes can also be discerned in the non-migrating birds.

Two other indigenous mammals to Cyprus were the dwart-hippopotamus (Hippopotamus fanurius) and the dwart-elephant (Elephas cyprius). These two species have today disappeared and the reason for their disappearance is attributed to man. These animals were the size of a pig, and similar to the types found on Crete, Corsica, Malta and other islands of the Agean. Indeed on all these islands where the elephant and hippopotamus populations were isloated after the Mediterranean was flooded, these species seem th have also undergone a similar evolution and deviation from their original species. Thus, the dwarf types evelved whic were suitable for survival in a more restricted natural habitat.

THE UNIFICATION OF THE TWO ISLANDS

The ascending movement of the two islands continued after the Mediterranean was once again filled. The result of this continuous rise of land was that the sea, which divided the two islands and which was shallow, soon became dry land and created the so called central plain or the Messaoria. This occured in the last 150.0000-100.000 years. Thus a natural land bridge was formed which enabled the migration of animals and plants from one island to the other and their proliferation on all of Cyprus. Some indigenous plants, however, still remain in their original habitat of Troodous and Pentadaktilou, because these two regions each have distinct rock and soil formations.

CLIMATE

The climate of Cyprus is considered a dry Mediterranean one with cold damp winters of short duration and dry, very hot summers of long duration. The mean average rainfall is about 500 mms. Most of the rainfalls occur between November and March.

Naturally the rainfall on the Troodos and the Pentadhactylos Ranges surpasses the mean rainfall; on the highest summit of the island, Mt. Chionistra, it may average up to 1000 mms. The least rain falls on the central plain, reaching a mere 254 mms in the west section in the region around Paphos.

The Troodos peaks are covered with snow in wintertime, and the highest points are snow-capped continually from December to the beginning of April, while on the northern side of Mt. Chionistra snow often remains as late as May.

VEGETATION AND FLORA

In antiquity the forests of Cyprus were far richer and more extended than they are today. According to what Eratosthenis (275-195 B.C.) says it is quite clear that the larger part of the island was at that time very well-wooded. Only one section of those forests exists at the present time. It is to be found chiefly in the Troodos and Pentadhactylos massifs covering just about 17%-18% of the terrain. The rest has disappeared through the activities of man whom, for centuries now has, by means of clearings and by fire, been trying to extend arable and grazing grounds to the detriment of the forest.

In the years prior to the Second World War the afforested area had fallen to an even lower level, mainly because of the unimpeded and irresponsible grazing of goats. Very drastic measures had to be taken, and co-ordinated efforts to be made by the then British administration for the renewal of the forests, either by natural regeneration or by re-

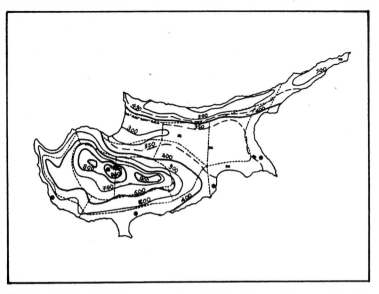

The mean average rainfall, in mms, in various districts of Cyprus. From the 1941-1970 records.

afforestation. The results of this policy, based largely on the ejection of the goats from the mountain zones can be plainly seen today, when one comes face to face with the splendid pine forests on the Troodos, and compares them with the denuded and arid mountains of Crete where irresponsibility and overgrazing are still the order of the day.

The British administration's policy was carried over later, after 1960, by the Cypriot Government. And it is a fact that fires rarely break out in the Cyprus forests because they are state-owned, consequently no private interests or claims exist.

However, the mistakes as well should be pointed out and stressed. The gravest of which is that during the last twenty years, clumps of trees and even whole forests have been planted consisting of species utterly foreign to the local vegetation. Such are different kinds of conifers and American sequoias in the highlands and diverse species of the Acacia genera and pines - such as Pinus halepensis (unknown as an indigenous tree in Cyprus) in the plains. Such errors should not be repeated in the future if we wish to preserve the ecological balance of the forests of Cyprus.

Starting from sea-level and climbing upwards towards the summits we ascertain the existence of distinct differences in the vegetation which occur in keeping with the altitude they are found growing at. But the rocks, too, play a definitive role in the type of vegetation found in each section, and in the species of trees, bushes or maquis that cover it.

The hills and the lower mountain zones were once covered with what is termed the

15

A Calabrian Pine (Pinus brutia) forest on the Troodos mountain.

"Mediterranean Maquis", and is composed of shrubs such as: Eastern or Strawberry Tree (Arbutus adrachne), Storax (Styrax officinalis), Wild Olive-trees (Olea europaea - subsp. oleaster), Kermes or Holly Oak (Quercus coccifera), or with hot climate trees, for instance Carob or Locust Tree (Ceratonia siliqua). Superb - shrub like this is preserved on the low northern slopes of the Pentadhactylos Range, at certain points of the lower zone of the Troodos Range and in the Akamas Peninsula as well as at divers localities of Karpassia. In other areas the original vegetation has given ground to the more grazing-resistant Phoenician Juniper (Juniperus phoenicea), to farmland, or to phrygana (Garrigue).

On the upper montane zone of the Pentadhactylos Range the predominant trees are the Calabrian Pines (Pinus brutia) species and native Cypresses (Cupressus sempervirens). At an altitude of about 600-1300 m. on the Troodos Range, Pinus brutia forms extensive forests, while the local oak (Quercus alnifolia) crops up here and there. Only in one certain locality, on the slopes of Tripylos Peak is there a forest of the endemic Cyprus Cedar (Cedrus libanii- subsp. brevifolia). However, afforestation using this species has been carried out at other points of the range too·

Climbing up to the highest Troodos zone we come across big forests of the Black Pine (Pinus nigra - subsp. pallasiana) which reach almost to the top of Chionistra Peak, an altitude of 1850 m. At certain places on the Troodos, the Madari and Papoutsa Peaks for instance, the Black Pine replaces Juniperus excelsa, while in the uppermost zone of Chionistra Peak we encounter a small Juniperus foetidissima wood.

In the Troodos gulleys and ravines grow the Plane Tree (Platanus orientalis), and the Asiatic
16   •

A Cedar forest on the Tripylos Peak.

species of Alder Alnus orientalis, while in the lower streams there is a profusion of the Oleander (Nerium oleander), and of the Chaste Tree (Vitex agnus-castus) shrubs.

The vegetation of the flats and the areas around salt-lakes has its own characteristics. The plants that grow there are hardy and salt-resistant. Instances are Salicornia fruticosa and Artiplex halimus, and, in combination with the sea, such as: Ferula communis and Cynara cardungulus, or even by semi-indigenous palms of the Phoenix dactylifera species.

Finally in the Central Plain wherever there is no farmland, there prevails a characteristic type of shrub, the preponderant plant being Crataegus azarolus. The same shrub can also be found in comparative abundance in the lower zone of the northern Troodos slopes.

The Cyprus flora is amongst the richest to be met with in the East Mediterranean countries, with 152 plant families, 660 genera, and about 1820 species many of which are endemic to the island, or else have but a very limited distribution in the East Mediterranean. Most of these plants are massed on the two mountain ranges, and in the Akamas Peninsula.

THE FAUNA IN THE PAST

There is historical evidence that in earlier ages there existed in Cyprus animals now extinct there. For instance, there is mention that wild pigs, wild goats, roe and deer, wild horses and

17

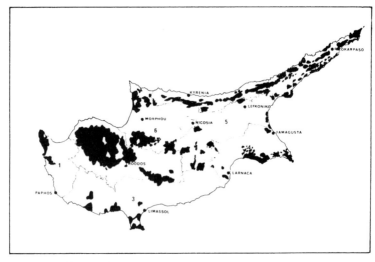

The forests of Cyprus today.

asses, and wild sheep roamed the Akamas Peninsula (see report on the protection of Akamas under the title of "Akamas: a heritage in danger" Nicosia 1987). Of the forementioned animals only the wild sheep continue to exist in Cyprus. We do not know exactly when each species of these animals disappeared, nor to which species they specifically belonged.

Taking into consideration the zoogeographical data we possess, however, we can assume that the wild pigs that once ranged over Cyprus belonged to the Sus scrofa species still to be found in the island's neighbouring countries, while the wild goats must have belonged to the Capra aegagrus, which species extends into western Asia and the Aegean, though it is not known whether some local subspecies might not have originated on the island. Finally, the roe must have been of the common European and western Asian species Capreolus capreolus.

As regards the other deer it is difficult to tell if they belonged to the common Euroasiatic Cervus elaphus or to Dama dama, the fallow deer, a truer Mediterranean species, which can even today be found in the adjacent island of Rhodes.

As to the wild horses and asses they seem more likely to have originated from erstwhile domesticated animals allowed to run wild. This occurrence in not unprecedented. It has happened on many islands of the eastern Mediterranean during the Middle Ages and the years of Turkish domination when the countryside was depopulated owing to the different invaders and to piratical incursions. (See author's book: "Greek Nature through the Ages",

A small bird caught on a lime-twig. Unfortunately this method of trapping birds is very widespread in Cyprus. (Photo by Friends of Earth).

Athens 1985).

The disappearance of all these large mammals is due solely to the activities of man. The two chief causes being shooting on the one hand, and the destruction of native habitats on the other.

SHOOTING AND POACHING

The killing of birds and mammals is a very widely-spread "Sport". We call it that because this activity has, of course, no connection with traditional shooting or hunting which in times past was practised for reasons of survival.

Within the Greek-Cypriot section of the island alone there are about 35.000 licensed hunters without counting all the unlicensed ones, or those who kill birds by means other than the gun and whose number it is very difficult to estimate. Equally unknown is the number of those who practise this sport in the occupied section of Cyprus.

19

Liming is an old traditional way of catching small birds in areas where many birds gather, such as wetlands. It has been calculated that nearly one person per family goes in for this sport. How detrimental this activity is to the avifauna can be seen from the following incident: in 1980 alone in the region of Paralimni, it is estimated that from 50,000 to 84,000 birds were caught.

Nets are another way of capturing birds. This method was unknown twenty years ago. Today it has greatly escalated as the nets are sold in increasingly larger numbers, together with fishing-nets. How catastrophic this way is can be seen from the fact that in Paralimni alone 84 birds got caught in one single day.

Shooting from inside cars, though illegal, is very widely practised. Another way is hunting by night using the car's headlights in the forests; this method too has gained many devotees. To this end the poachers use the dense network of roads found on all the mountains on the island.

Finally, the problem rests on the number of legal and illegal sportsmen, a number that is too large in proportion to the total area of the island on the one hand, and with its population of birds and mammals on the other. It is characteristic that on the first day of the turtle-dove shooting season, more than 1000 sportsmen were stationed round Lake Almiri at Akrotiri, awaiting the coming of the turtle-doves. In the same year, and on the first day of the autumn shooting season of turtle-doves the sportsmen who had gathered at Fassouri killed in addition all the water-birds that were there.

Unfortunately there are no statistics, but it has been estimated that if every Cypriot sportsman kills only 30 small and large birds per year, then over a million are slaughtered in that period of time. Naturally we are not taking into account the mammals killed. No systematic observations have as yet been carried out on them.

MEASURES TAKEN FOR THE PROTECTION OF THE FAUNA

One of the principal measures taken for the protection of the fauna is the existence of extensive belts where shooting is strictly prohibited all the year round, largely in mountain zones. Such "reservation belts" were first established mainly to protect wild sheeps, partridges, francolins, and hares that they might breed in safety. On the whole, mountain reservations are respected by sportsmen perhaps because it is not easy for them to do any shooting there without being spotted. On the contrary on wetland reservations there is systematic poaching going on.

Another protective measure is to forbid all shooting from January 1 to September 30. This would be a most effective measure were there no exceptions to it. Many sportsmen use these exceptions as an excuse for wholesale slaughter. Here is an example: from the middle of April to the middle of May is the 'spring turtle-dove shooting season'. This is prohibited over almost the whole of Europe. The end result is that not only several thousands of turtle-doves are needlessly killed but so are many other birds whose breeding season this happens to be.

For the effectual protection of the fauna it is imperative that the following steps be taken: a) the spring shooting season to be entirely discontinued; b) the wetlands rigorously protected; c) the sale of lime-twigs and nets strictly outlawed; and d) the mountain reserves better supervised.

The four areas in Cyprus which are of vital ecological importance are: 1) the Larnaca salt lakes; 2) the Limassol salt lakes; 3) the Akamas Peninsula; and, lastly, the Karpas Peninsula in the territory occupied by the Turks.

The great importance Cyprus has as a resting-place for migratory birds can be seen from the map showing their migration routes.

Swallows (Hirundo rustica) gathered on wires in readiness for the autumn migration to Africa.

THE BIRDS

Cyprus is well-known for its wealth of avifauna embracing as it does 340 species in all. This incredible richness of species is due in the first place largely to the fact that the island is a transit point for the migratory birds coming down from the north in winter or up from Africa in spring.

Only 46 species reside permanently in Cyprus, while 27 species of the migratory birds nest and breed on the island. To the latter another 24 species of the migrants should be added, these nest and breed only occasionally. The remaining 243 species come to Cyprus either as winter visitors or simply pass over as they migrate. Among them are those that appear only accidentally.

The areas in Cyprus where the birds are most plentiful is in the forests of the great Troodos Range. That is where one comes across the Chaffinch (Fringilla coelebs), the Cyprus Crossbill (Loxia curvirostra-guillemardi), the Cyprus Partridge (Alectoris chukar-cypriotis), the Short-toed Treecreeper (Certhia brachydactyla), the Spotted Flycatcher (Muscicapa striata) the Coal Tit (Parus ater), the Nightingale (Luscinia megarhynchos), the Wren (Troglodytes troglodytes), the Cyprus Pied Wheatear (Oenanthe cypriaca), Cetti's Warbler (Cettia cetti), the Masked Shrike (Lanius nubicus), the Jay (Garrulus Glandarius) and many more sylvan and mountain species.

The last few pairs of Black Vultures (Aegypius monachus) and of Imperial Eagles (Aquila helica) nest on the same range. Both species are threatened with extinction.

On the much lower and less wooded Pentadhactylos Range there are Griffon Vultures (Gyps fulvus) and it is probable that a few pairs of Bonelli's Eagles (Hieratus fasciatus) still nest there. On this same range we can meet other interesting birds too, for instance Woodpigeons (Columba palumbus), Alpine Swifts (Apus melba), Crag Martins (Ptyonoprogne (hirundo) rupestris), Blue Rock Thrushes (Monticola solitarius), and many more.

Resident species not restricted only to mountain regions, that is to say, enjoying a wider distribution, are the Cyprus Partridge or Chukar (Alectoris chukar-cypriotis), the Kestrel (Falco tinunculus), the Scops Owl (Otus scops), the Little Owl (Athene noctua), the Great Tit (Parus major), the House Sparrow (Passer domesticus), the Corn Bunting (Miliaria emberiza calandra), the Crested Lark (Galerida cristata), etc. The once common Black Francolin or Black Partridge (Francolinus francolinus), today is restricted to the two opposite ends of Cyprus, namely, to the Carpas and the Akamas Peninsulas.

The most numerous migrants nesting in Cyprus are Swallows (Hirundo rustica), House Martins (Delichon urbica), Olivaceous Warblers (Hippolais pallida), Swifts (Apus apus), Pallid Swifts (Apus pallidus), among others. Less common are Turtle Doves (Streptopelia turtur), Nightjars (Caprimulgus europeaeus), Hoopees (Upupa epops), Rollers (Coracias garrulus), Bee-eaters (Merops apiaster) and others. There are also a few pairs of Yellow Wagtails (Motacilla flava), and a few Golden Orioles (Oriolus oriolus), and circa 100 pairs of Eleonora's Falcons (Falco eleonorae) found on rocky coasts in the south of the island.

Few of the marshland birds stop to breed in Cyprus, though in favourable years the number of breeding species increases rapidly. It should, however, be noted that a few decades ago when the wetlands in Cyprus had not as yet been seriously disturbed by man, many more species of aquatic birds used to breed there.

In earlier times, when Cyprus was a forest-clad island, the mountain species must have been far more numerous. Besides, the change in the vegetation did not leave uninfluenced the behaviour of many species. Thus Falco naumanni (Lesser Kestrel) and Cinclus cinclus (Dipper) no longer breed in Cyprus. The population of other species again - such as the Cyprus Partridge, the Francolin, the Vulture and some others - are far fewer than they used to be.

On the other hand the creation of conditions leading to isolation in many of the lowland zones has favoured other species, such as the Stone Curlew (Burhinus cedicnemus), the Calandra Lark (Melanocorypha calandra), the Black-bellied Sandgrouse (Pterocles orientalis) to name but a few. An interesting fact well worth noting is that two species which formerly did not exist in Cyprus or else appeared rarely have these latter years formed permanent colonies and spread out over several areas. These two species are the Greenfinch (Carduelis chloris) and a species of Sparrow - the Dead Sea Sparrow (Passer moabiticus).

It is remarkable, too, that many endemic birds exist on the island, not found anywhere else - to cite some: Otus scops - cyprius (Cyprus Scops Owl), Oenanthe pleschanka - cypriaca (Cyprus Pied Wheatear). Parus ater-cypriotes (Cyprus Coal Tit), Certhia brachydactyla - dorotheae (Cyprus Short-toed Treecreeper), Loxia curvirostra-guillemardi (Crossbill), Garrulus glandarius-glaszner (Glaszner's Jay) and many others. If we take into consideration the proximity of Cyprus with the Middle East countries the number of endemic subspecies or genera is regarded as a large one.

Some of the species of the birds in Cyprus mentioned in this book are, unfortunately, on the brink of disappearing while others have not been seen for the last 5-10 years. The basic reasons for this state of affairs are two: a) the merciless shooting that goes on and b) the destruction of the birds' natural habitat.

Unfortunately, no attempt has been made so far to establish common Cypriot bird-names. As a matter of fact the Cypriot ornithologists make use of the common English names.

Accipitridae Family

Diurnal, carnivorous birds of prey, feeding on live animals or carrion. Bills are hooked at the tip, and so are their talons to some extent.

1. Gyps fulvus (Griffon Vulture)

A large bird similar to the eagle, neck and head covered with thick short white down. The rest of the body is covered with fuscous feathers. The wingspan is 230-280 cms. The length of its body 100-110 cms. It feeds on carcasses only, mainly on the entrails. It nests in small colonies on precipitous cliffs. It lays a single egg in February.

This used to be a common species all over Cyprus, today it is restricted to only a few localities, and nests solely in the Episcopi area. Vultures have also been observed passing over Cyprus as migrants.

2. Aegypius monachus (Black Vulture)

Very similar to 1, but its colour is black. In size they are the same. Earlier on there were several in the Troodos forests, but today they have disappeared.

3. Gypaetus barbatus-aureus (Lammergeier, Bearded Vulture)

This is the largest bird in Cyprus. It measures 110-150 cms. from tip to tail, with a 235-265 cm, wingspan. It resembles a vulture but its tail is wedge-shaped at the tip. Its head and neck have a richer plumage. Eyes reddish surrounded by small black feathers. At the base of the bill it has two tufts of black hairs like a moustache. It is fulvous on the head, neck, breast, belly and feet. The wings, back, and tail are dark brown. It lays two eggs every January. Usually it is the stronger of the two chicks that survives. It feeds on carcasses, and chiefly on bones which it swallows whole or, if too large, breaks by dropping from a height on to rocks. Following flocks of sheep it also eats the afterbirth of the ewes. This bird does not reside permanently in Cyprus but appears occasionally and accidentally coming from neighbouring countries. Evidently nowadays the conditions on the mountains of Cyprus, such as the lack of stock-breeding, do not allow it to establish itself there permanently.

4. Neophron percnopterus (Egyptian Vulture)

A small Vulture, which when in flight resembles a stork in size and colour. It measures - tip to tail - only 65 cms. It feeds on carcasses, rubbish and small animals. It passes through Cyprus only on its migrations.

5. Aquila chrysaetos (Golden Eagle)

Length up to 97 cms., and wingspan up to 227 cms. Dark brown colour, lighter on neck and head. Square tail. Fully-feathered legs. Bill and toes yellowish. It nests on rocks and builds two or three nests which it uses in rotation. It usually lays two eggs about the end of February. It feeds on small animals, birds and tortoises, much more rarely on carcasses. A rare accidental visitor to Cyprus.

6. Aquila heliaca (Imperial Eagle)

Similar to 5 but somewhat smaller in size, with 2 characteristic white patches on the back at the base of the wings. In former times it was common to the mountains of Cyprus. Today rare, and only on the Pentadhactylos Range.

Black Vulture

Lammergeier

Golden Eagle

Imperial Eagle (juvenile)

7. Aquila clanga (Spotted Eagle)

Similar to the Golden Eagle but only 62-66 cms. in length. The plumage of the immature birds is mottled white. It nests in forests. An accidental visitor to Cyprus.

8. Aquila pomarina (Lesser Spotted Eagle)

This is the smallest of the Aquila genus of eagles. 54-60 cms. It is like 7 but the immature individuals have fewer white spots. A passage migrant over Cyprus.

9. Hieratus pennatus (Booted Eagle)

Smaller than 8 (45-54 cms. in length). Wingspan 110-132 cms. Upper parts of adults greyish-brown and whitish or chestnut with darker spots on breast and belly. A rare, passage migrant.

10. Hieratus fasciatus (Bonelli's Eagle)

Similar to 9 but larger, reaching 65-75 cms. in length, and with a wingspan of 150-170 cms. Adults blackish-brown above and whitish underneath, with characteristic black bars at tip of tail. There are individuals which are brown underneath. However, both the lighter-coloured and the darker-coloured individuals have black spots on the breast. A rare permanent resident of the Cyprus mountains. Formerly it was common.

11. Circaetus gallicus (Short-toed Eagle).

Similar to 10 but above a greyish-brown and beneath whitish, either spotted or not. Legs half-feathered. Length 64-72 cms., wingspan 160-180 cms. A rare passage migrant.

12. Buteo buteo (Common Buzzard).

Quite a large bird of prey with bare yellowish lower legs. Brown above and paler underneath with thick dark spots. There are light-coloured individuals also. Length 52-54 cms. Wingspan 118-140 cms. Nests in trees in open woods. Catches rodents, reptiles, and ground birds. A common passage migrant which flies over Cyprus every spring and autumn in large flocks.

13. Buteo rufinus (Long-legged Buzzard)

Like 13 but somewhat larger and more reddish in colour. Nests among rocks and hunts in open dry localities. Feeds on small mammals, reptiles, and insects. A rare winter visitor.

14. Buteo lagopus (Rough-legged Buzzard)

Similar to 12 but a little larger, mottled greyish-brown to grey in colour, fully-feathered legs. Feeds on small mammals. A passage winter visitor.

15. Pernis apivorus (Honey Buzzard)

Similar to the other buzzards but smaller, about 55 cms. long. Colour very variable, though usually the upper part is dark chestnut, the head grey, and the underparts light-coloured with dark spots. Rather a common passage migrant, especially in spring.

16. Milvus milvus (Red Kite)

A characteristic swallow-tailed bird of prey of medium size (50-60 cms). Generally brown in colour, breast more rufous, head lighter-coloured. It feeds on small animals, rubbish, insects, and carrion. A rare passage visitor.2

17. Milvus migrans (Black Kite)

Like 16 but slightly smaller, darker-coloured and very slightly swallow-tailed. Quite a common passage migrant.

18. Haliaetus albicilla (White-tailed Eagle)

Like the Golden Eagle in size and colour but its tail is slightly wedge-shapod, and in adults

Lesser Spotted Eagle

Bonelli's Eagle

Common Buzzard

Honey Buzzard

white underneath. It usually nests in large trees near coastal wetlands and feeds on fish, sick or wounded birds, and carrion. It is a very rare bird and appears in Cyprus sporadically, either as a winter visitor or as a passage migrant.

19. Accipiter gentilis (Goshawk)

A medium-sized bird of prey, 49-61 cms. in length, and with a wingspan of 100-120 cms. Tail relatively long, legs featherless. Greyish-brown to black above and white below with thick dark spots. Spots a characteristic white bar above its eyes. Lays 3-4 eggs every April. Nests in trees in dense forests, and feeds on birds and small creatures. A rare species for Cyprus. Probably a few pairs reside permanently in the forest of the Troodos Range where the species has been observed.

20. Accipiter nisus (Sparrowhawk)

Like 19 but smaller, 31-38 cms. long and 60-80 cms. in wingspan. The male is smaller in size than the female, breast redder, and reddish behind the eye. It frequents open woods, feeding on small birds, insects, or more rarely, on small mammals. A passage migrant and winter visitor.

21. Accipiter brevipes (Levant Sparrowhawk)

Similar to 19 and 20 but of an in-between size (33-38cms). The male resembles the sparrowhawk in colour. The female is darker on top. A rare bird of passage.

22. Circus aeruginosus (Marsh Harrier)

A medium-sized bird of prey with a long and narrow tail. The over-all colour is chestnut. In the males the tail and part of the wings are greyish-white. Length 49-56 cms. Wingspan 116-130 cms. Nests on the ground in reed beds, and feeds on marsh birds and animals. Either a passage migrant, or a winter visitor.

23. Circus cyaneus (Hen Harrier)

Similar to the former but smaller - sized (43-50 cms). The female is brown with a darkly barred tail; the male grey with wing edges black. Nests in marshes. A passage migrant, and winter visitor.

24. Circus macrourus (Pallid Harrier)

A dimorphic species similar to the Hen Harrier. The male is light grey on the upper part and almost white on the lower. The female is almost identical with the corresponding female of the Hen Harriers. A migrant bird of passage.

25. Circus pygargus (Montagu's Harrier)

A dimorphic species like the Hen Harrier but smaller in size. The male has a white belly with vertical rufous streaks. A rare bird of passage.

Pandionidae Family

Diurnal birds of prey. They reside near the sea or brackish lakes and feed on fish.

1. Pandion Haliaetus (Osprey)

Length 51-58 cms. Wingspan 151-188 cms. Dark brown on back and wings, white underneath and on head. A characteristic band behind the eyes which continues down to the neck. Nests in trees, and feeds on fish. A rare passage migrant.

Falconidae Family

Rapacious diurnal birds of relatively small size, feeding invariably on live prey.

Black Kit

Goshawk

Marsh Harrier

Eleonara's Falcon

1. Falco peregrinus-subspecies brookei (Peregrine)

A very well-known hawk, widely distributed. Length 38-50 cms. Wingspan 83-113 cms. Dark grey almost black, whitish-fawn on wings and back, with thick small dark specks on belly, breast, and leg feathers. Wings narrow. Nests on precipitous crags. Feeds on birds it strikes in the air. In a steep swoop it can develop a speed up to 400 km. per hour. It lays 3-4 eggs. Today a rare species. Only a few pairs reside permanently in Cyprus; others are observed passing through during their migration.

2. Falco eleonorae (Eleonora's Falcon)

Similar to 1 but the all-over colour is darker while the underparts are more rufous. There are also individuals that are entirely one-coloured: black. About 38 cms. in length. It nests in flocks on the cliffs of precipitous coasts and on rocky islets around Cyprus. Feeds on

29

insects, small creatures, small reptiles and birds it catches during their migrations. Breeds in Cyprus. In wintertime it migrates to Africa.

3. Falco subbuteo (Hobby)

Like 1 but smaller (30-36 cms in length). Legs and underside of belly reddish. A passage migrant.

4. Falco columbarius (Merlin)

A small hawk, 27-33 cms. in length. Underparts fuscous with dark specks. Back in female brown, in male grey; head a dull yellow with darker specks. A rare bird of passage or winter visitor.

5. Falco tinunculus (Kestrel)

Relatively small, around 34 cms in length. The female's back, head, and tail are brown with black specks. Her breast and belly fulvous with dark specks. The male is similar but for head and tail which are grey. Both sexes have a characteristic black vertical streak under the eye. Nests on rocks and lays 4-5 eggs at the end of March. Feeds on rodents, reptiles, insects, and small birds. A common permanent Cyprus resident.

6. Falco naumanni (Lesser Kestrel)

Like 5 but smaller (30cms. in length). The female almost identical with the female of 5. The male is brown on the back, unspotted, wings grey with black edges, head and tail grey. A very useful bird to man; it used to live in colonies in old houses. It feeds on insects, rodents, lizards, frogs, etc. At the present time it appears in Cyprus only as a passing migrant, whereas formerly it resided there during the summer months.

7. Falco vespertinus (Red-footed Falcon)

This is a bird with strong sexual dimorphism. The male is greyish-black except for the plumage of legs and belly which is reddish. The female is grey with black specks on the back, and brown with sparse black streaks on the underparts. The female's head is reddish and the throat whitish while under the eye there is a vertical streak. Length of both sexes about 30 cms. A common passage bird.

8. Falco cherrug (Saker Falcon)

A large hawk about the same size as 1 (circa 46 cms). It can be distinguished by its colouring. The head, breast, belly, and legs are whitish, mottled with sparse dark specks (in immature birds the specks are thicker). The top side is a greyish-brown mottled black. The tail grey with darker stripes. Male and female almost the same. A passage migrant.

9. Falco concolor (Sooty Falcon)

A small hawk, generally greyish-black or sometimes entirely black. An African species. A very rare visitor to Cyprus.

Hobby

Kestrel

Lesser Kestrel

Red-footed Falcon

Strigidae Family

Rapacious nocturnal birds with hooked nails and bill. When standing 2 talons are turned forwards and 2 backwards. The head is large, round, with eyes to the front. Often these are 2 short or long tufts of feathers which give one the impression that they are ears.

1. Asio otus (Long-eared Owl)

A medium-sized owl, 35-38 cms. in length and a 85-100 cms. wingspan. Tawny-coloured or a greyish-fawn with dark downstrokes. Belly lighter. Two tufts on head. Eyes yellow. Haunts olive-groves and clumps of trees. Eats small mammals it catches at night. Lays 4-7 eggs every April in other birds' nests. Not very common but, in any case, a species that remains and breeds in Cyprus.

31

2. Asio flammeus (Short-eared Owl)

Like 1 but browner, slightly larger and 'ears' much smaller, just visible. A rare migrant or winter visitor.

3. Otus scops subsp. cyprius (Scops Owl of Cyprus)

Similar to 1 but smaller (18-20cms) with dark and white specks. Tufts medium. Lays 3-4 eggs end of April. Feeds on insects and, more rarely, on small rodents and birds. Nests in hollows of trees or walls. Usually a bird of passage in Cyprus, but most probably a few pairs remain on the island and breed.

4. Athene noctua (Little Owl)

A small tuftless Owl. Greyish-brown, breast lighter. White spots on wings and dark ones on breast. Eats small rodents, insects, lizards, worms and small birds. Nests in tree hollows, or holes in walls. In April it lays 3-6 eggs. Dwells in olive-groves, sparse woods, and gardens. A common resident species 22 cms.

Tytonidae Family

Nocturnal birds of prey similar to Owls.

1. Tyto alba subsp. erlangeri (Barn Owl)

A pretty bird with golden-grey plumage above, and golden with dark specks beneath. Length circa 34 cms. Nests in ruins, stables and so forth. Hunts in open spaces. Lays 4-7 eggs every April, and sometimes breeds for a second time in summer.

Ardeidae Family

Birds with more or less long, pointed necks and long slender legs. They live in wet places, wading in shallow water in search of their food. Neck retracted in flight gives them a figure 5 silhouette.

1. Ardea cinerea (Grey Heron)

A long, white-necked and yellow-billed bird. Breast and belly white. Back grey. A characteristic black band extends from eyes and terminates in two bandlike feathers. Length 90 cm. A common passage migrant. Occasionally a few of these birds winter in Cyprus.

2. Ardea purpurea (Purple Heron)

Practically similar to 1 but with neck, breast and belly rufous. Length circa 78 cms. A very common bird of passage.

3. Egretta alba (Great White Egret)

Similar to the two former birds but white with black bill and legs. At breeding time the bill and legs turn yellow at their base, while a tuft of long ornamental plumes grows on back. Length 90 cms. A rare passage migrant.

Long-eared Owl

Little Owl

Grey Heron

Little Egret

4. Egretta garzetta (Little Egret)

Almost identical with 3 but much smaller in size (56 cms), and with yellow feet. A common bird of passage. Very rarely do some remain over summer in Cyprus to breed.

5. Bubulcus ibis (Cattle Egret)

A medium-sized (51 cms) bird with reddish legs and a not very long neck. In colour very pale beige, with head and breast a darker beige. Bill yellow. A rare bird of passage.

6. Ardeola ralloides (Squacco Heron)

Very similar to 5 but darker and smaller (length 46 cms) Legs green. Bill green with a black tip. On crown a crest of bandlike feathers falling back. A common passage migrant.

7. Nycticorax nycticorax (Night Heron)

Similar to 5 and 6 in outline, but larger (61 cms). White underneath and black on top. Wings and tail grey. Bill blackish and legs yellowish. A common passage migrant. On rare occasions a few nest on the island.

8. Ixobrychus minutus (Little Bittern)

Like, the Night Heron but smaller (35 cms) with beige underparts. Wings beige and black. Tail black. Quite a common passage bird.

9. Botaurus stellaris (Bittern)

Similar to the Night Heron in outline but larger (76 cms). All-over colour beige-brown darkly mottled. On the whole a rare bird of passage.

Ciconiidae Family

Birds very like Egrets but they do not retract necks to form the figure 5 when in flight, on the contrary they fly with outstretched necks.

1. Ciconia ciconia (White Stork)

102 cms. in length. The whole body is white except for the wings which are a combination of white and black. Bill and legs orange. As a passage migrant it is quite a common bird.

2. Ciconia nigra (Black Stork)

Identical with 1 but somewhat smaller (97 cms) and black, save for underparts which are white. Not a usual migrant.

Thresciornidae Family

Wading birds, in appearance similar to the Egrets and Storks but with bill to some extent hooked; in rarer cases straight and flat at tip.

1. Plegadis falcinellus (Glossy Ibis)

Reddish .brown in colour. Long, curved grey bill. Grey legs. 56 cms in length. Quite a common bird of passage.

2. Platalea leucorodia (Spoonbill)

A white-bodied bird with legs and bill black. Bill straight and spoon-shaped at tip. Rather a rare bird of passage.

Phoenicopteridae Family

Large birds with very long legs and a very long neck, and with a characteristic bill,

Night Heron.

White Stork.

Black Stork.

Glossy Ibis.

short and thick curving abruptly downwards at the tip. They live in brackish waters.

1. Phoenicopterus ruber - subsp. roseus (Greater Flamingo)

Pink all over. Wings in flight dark pink and black. A reddish, black-tipped bill. Red legs. Length of body 127 cms. Large flocks winter in Cyprus, mainly by the salt lake of Akrotiri. They are also quite common as birds of passage.

Anatidae Family

Aquatic birds with more or less long necks and short legs. Feet webbed. Short bill, flattened at tip and thick at base. Males often many-coloured. Females generally more uniform in colour.

35

1. Cygnus olor (Mute Swan)

Large long-necked white bird. Bill orange, with black basal knob in front of eyes. Fee blackish. Juveniles grey. 152 cms. in length. A rare winter visitor to the island's sa lakes.

2. Cygnus cygnus (Whooper Swan)

Like 1 but bill yellowish turning black towards tip, without knob in front of eyes. A very rare accidental visitor.

3. Anser anser (Greylag Goose)

This bird resembles a farmyard goose. Grey in colour, legs and bill orange. 76-89 cms. i length. An accidental winter visitor.

4. Anser albifrons (White-fronted Goose)

It is very like 3 but its general colouring is darker, its legs yellowish, and between the bil and the eyes there is a narrow white band. Length 66-76 cms. Rather a rare winte visitor.

5. Alopochen aegyptiacus (Egyptian Goose)

The all-over colour is beige, while the back is light -brown or grey. The wings in flight are three-coloured: white, black and green. Bill and legs pink. 70 cms in length. Formerly a frequent winter visitor. This species was last observed in Cyprus in 1968.

6. Tadorna ferruginea (Ruddy Shelduck)

Like 5 but general colouring darker beige-brown. Length 64 cms. Legs and bill black. This species appears in Cyprus in winter, not every year however.

7. Tadorna tadorna (Shelduck)

Similar to 5 and 6 in appearance, but very different as regards colour. The general colour is white with a chestnut breastband. Head dark-green. Wings white and black. Bill and legs pink The drake has a characteristic red knob at the base of its bill. 61 cms in length. A common winter visitor.

```
1  | 2
   |
   |- - - -
   | 3
   |
4  | 5
   |
```

1.Greater Flamingo, 2.Mute Swans, 3.Greylag Goose
4.Ruddy Shelduck, 5.Shelduck

8. Anas platyrhynchos (Mallard)

Like the farmyard duck whose wild ancestor it is. The drake is grey with a dark-green head and neck, and a rufous breast. The tail has two upturned feathers curling backwards. The female is a uniform greyish-beige with darker specks. Length 58 cms. A common winter visitor and autumn bird of passage. Occasionally a few pairs stay on in summer too, and breed on the island during the spring months.

9. Anas strepera (Gadwall)

Like 8 but smaller (51cms). The duck is almost identical with the Mallard female. The drake differs from No 8 drake in the colour of the head and breast which are grey. This species appears sporadically in Cyprus either as a bird of passage or as a winter visitor.

10. Anas penelope (Wigeon)

Like Nos. 8 and 9, but smaller still (46 cms). Duck a uniform greyish-beige. The drake resembles a mallard but with head, throat and breast chestnut. Crown yellowish. A common bird of passage especially in autumn, and a regular winter visitor.

11. Anas querquedula (Garganey)

A small duck 38 cms. long. Duck one colour like the ducks of the other species. Drake's belly and flanks are light grey, head light brown with a conspicuous stripe from eyes down to nape. A common passage migrant.

12. Anas crecca (Teal)

Like 11 but smaller (35cms). Drake's head is chestnut with a distinctive broad green stripe. The tail coverts are yellowish and encircled by a black band. A very common winter visitor.

13. Anas clypeata (Shoveler)

It differs from the other wild ducks by its bill which is longer and flattened at tip like a shovel. In colour the duck resembles the ducks of the other species. The drake has a green head, white breast, rufous belly and a black mantle. The wings are blue at base. 51 cms. long. A common winter visitor. It is also common as a bird of passage, especially in spring.

14. Anas acuta (Pintail)

The drake differs from the other drakes by the two greatly elongated central tail feathers. In colour the duck is like the other wild ducks. Drake generally light grey with head chestnut throat white and mantle black. Bill greyish-green. Length 56 cms. Very common winter visitor and passage migrant, especially in spring.

Mallard.

Wigeon.

Teal.

Shoveler.

15. Marmaronetta (Anas) angustirostris (Marbled Teal)

The only wild duck where both sexes are of the same colour. The over-all colour is beige with darker and lighter speckles on back and flanks. On the head there is a characteristic crest of long feathers. Length 41 cms. In former times it was quite common and probably nested on Cyprus. Today it appears but very rarely.

16. Netta rufina (Red-crested Pochard)

This is one of the most beautiful of the wild ducks. The drake has a red head and bill, a black throat and breast, a black tail, flanks and belly light grey and a greyish-brown back. Duck is pale beige on back with a greyish-brown crown. Length 56 cms. A rare winter visitor.

17. Aythya marila (Scaup)

Duck is a dark beige-grey with a white band round bill. Drake's head is dark green, breast and tail black, belly and flanks a light grey, and a dark grey back. 48 cms. in length. A rare winter visitor.

18. Aythya fuligula (Tufted Duck)

Similar to 17 but smaller (43 cms). The duck is darker without a white band round bill. The drake has on its head a characteristic drooping black crest. Back black. A rare winter visitor.

19. Aythya ferina (Pochard)

Similar to 17 but the drake's head is chestnut. The duck has no white band round the bill. Length 46 cms. Quite a common winter visitor.

20. Aythya nyroca (Ferruginous Duck)

Duck greyish-black except for lower belly which is white. Drake is chestnut with greyish-black back and tail. 41 cms. in length. A rare passage migrant or winter visitor.

21. Melanita nigra (Common Scoter)

Drake all black, bill yellowish with black basal knob. Duck greyish-black, cheeks light grey. 48 cms. long. Very rare accidental visitor.

22. Bucephala clangula (Golden-eye)

A medium-sized bird with a big head, duck's brown, drake's green. The rest of the body grey. The back, tail and part of the wings of drake black. Length 42 cms. Accidental winter visitor.

23. Oxyura leucocephala (White-headed Duck)

A strange bird with quite a long pointed tail, and a very thick blue bill. The all-over colour of both sexes is brown, but the drake's face is white with a black band going over crown, and a black collar. When swimming, the drakes raise their tails. (46 cms. in length). A rare winter visitor.

24. Mergus merganser (Goosander)

A large bird, 58-66 cms., with a relatively slender bill, abruptly hooked at tip. Duck grey with chestnut head ornamented with two small crests. Drake white with a blackish back and a crestless dark green head. A rare winter visitor.

25. Mergus serrator (Red-breasted Merganser)

Like 24 but smaller (53-58 cms). Duck almost identical with that of 24. Drake is light grey,

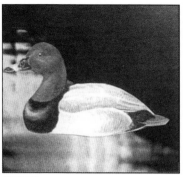

Pochard

Golden-eye

White-headed Duck

Goosander

with green crested head, white collar at throat, and breast with dark speckles. A rare winter visitor.

26. Mergus albellus (Smew)

This species is very different from the former species. In the male the general colour is white, the tail grey, the back and the wing tips blackish. The head feathers are somewhat puffed giving the appearance of a rudimentary crest. At the back of the head there is a black line and a black patch round each eye. The female is light grey with the top of the head brown. Length 41 cms. An occasional winter visitor.

Rallidae Family

Water fowl with a short tail, a slender pointed bill, and quite long legs. Long toes, sometimes flattened at sides into fleshy lobes.

1. Rallus aquaticus (Water Rail)

A bird similar to a woodcock but smaller (28cms). Plumage grey mottled black on upper-parts, unmottled on breast, throat and head, belly striped black. Bill reddish and quite long. A rather common passage bird and winter visitor.

2. Porzana porzana (Spotted Crake)

Similar to 1 but smaller (23 cms) and more mottled. Short-billed. Quite common as a passage migrant, especially in spring.

3. Porzana Parva (Little Crake)

Similar to 1 but only 19 cms long and with a short bill. A common passage migrant, especially in spring.

4. Porzana pusilla (Baillon's Crake)

Similar to 1 but short-billed and only 18 cms. long. A rare bird of passage. Occasionally a few pairs nest on Cyprus.

5. Crex crex (Corncrake)

Like the Spotted Crake in appearance but larger (27 cms). All-over colour beige-brown. Black spotted mantle, belly with brown stripes. A rare passage migrant.

6. Fulica atra (Coot)

A 38 cms. long black body. Thick grey legs with fleshy lobes on toes. Bill white with a white patch on forehead. A passage bird and winter visitor. Very few birds of this species remain in Cyprus to breed.

7. Gallinula chloropus (Moorhen)

Very like 6 but smaller (33cms), with a little white on the tail. Legs greenish. Toes without lobes. Bill reddish, green at tip. A passage migrant and winter visitor.

8. Porphyrula alleni (Allen's Gallinule)

Like 7 but smaller (24 cms). Reddish legs. Bill reddish with a whitish extension to forehead. Accidental, rare visitor.

Water Rail.

Little Crake.

Coot.

Moorhen.

9. Porphyrio porphyrio (Purple or Green-backed Gallinule)

Similar to 7 and 8 but a larger bird, about 48 cms. in length. Blue-black. Strong bill red with red extension on forehead. A rare accidental visitor.

Gruidae Family

Large birds resembling storks, but on the whole with a short bill. With a large tuft of ornamental plumes hanging from back towards tail.

1. Grus grus (Common Crane)

Colour grey. White neck and black throat. Head black and white with a red spot on crown.

114 cms. in length. A quite common bird of passage that flies in large flocks over Cyprus every spring and autumn.

2. Anthropoides virgo (Demoiselle Crane)

Like 1 but smaller (96 cms). Head and neck black. From the throat there hangs a tuft of black feathers towards breast. White ear-tufts start from behind each eye. A common enough passage migrant.

Caprimulgidae Family

Nocturnal insectivore birds with a weak thin bill and small slender legs.

1. Caprimulgus europaeus (Nightjar)

A bird whose greyish-brown colouring makes it difficult to distinguish from the earth or tree branches. Length about 27 cms. Tail long and slender. Voice insistent and shrill. A common passage bird, rarely remaining in Cyprus to nest in summer.

Phasianidae Family

Birds with a short thick body, short triangular bill, slightly hooked at tip; jaunty gait; short wings. In many species the males are many-coloured. Almost all nest on ground.

1. Alectoris chukar - subsp. cypriotes (Cyprian Chukar)

A short-tailed bird; legs and bill reddish; mantle grey; belly beige vertically barred on flanks; breast and throat a pale whitish beige ringed by a black band commencing at eyes. Male and female practically identical. Length 33 cms. It nests in the undergrowth of the Troodos forests and in rocky localities. A quite common endemic Cyprus bird.

2. Francolinus francolinus (Black Francolin)

Similar to a partridge in size and outline, but very differently coloured. The female is black-speckled grey-brown while the male has a black belly, breast and head, a golden-brown back, a reddish collar, and white specks on flanks. It also has two characteristic white spots on the head behind the eyes. It is a West-Asian species once very populous in Cyprus. Today it can be found nesting on the Carpassia and Akames peninsulas as well as in the Akrotiri area.

3. Coturnix coturnix (Quail)

It looks like a small partridge; its length is 18 cms. Its colour is grey-fawn with darker specks. In the male the throat is black and ringed with a white and black band. Populations of this species are permanent residents in Cyprus. They nest in fields, maquis, and bushes. Large flocks pass over the island in spring and autumn during their migrations.

Common Crane

Nighjar

Black Francolin

Great Crested Grebe

Podicepidae Family

Aquatic birds with a slender, sharp bill, quite a long neck, head either with a crest or without one, and toes with fleshy lobes which help them to swim.

1. Podiceps cristatus (Great Crested Grebe)

Mantle grey, belly, breast and throat almost white. A double crest on crown of head, and feather protuberances on the anterior flanks. These characteristics, however, common to both sexes, practically disappear in wintertime. Length 48 cms. This species lives by lakes, marshes and lagoons. A passage migrant or winter visitor. In former times small populations nested in Cyprus.

2. Podiceps grisegena (Red-necked Grebe)

Similar to 1 but smaller (43 cms), with darker colours, chestnut neck and smaller crests. In winter almost identical in colour with 1. A rare accidental winter visitor.

3. Podiceps auritus (Slavonian Grebe)

Like 1 and 2 in winter but much smaller, only 33 cms in length. In summer brown with palerbelly and darker mantle. Head blackish with brown crests. A rare, accidental winter visitor.

4. Podiceps nigricolis (Black-necked Grebe)

Like 3 but smaller (30 cms) and with a black neck. In winter similar in colour to the other species. A common winter visitor.

5. Tachybaptus ruficolis (Little Grebe)

The smallest species of the family. It loocks like a duckling (27 cms). In summer the general colour is grey, the back blackish, the neck brown and the head black. In winter it turns a much paler grey. A common enough passage bird and winter visitor.

Procellariidae Family

Long-feathered seabirds which glide as they fly very near the surface of the sea, covering long distances. Feet webbed.

1. Calonectris diomedea (Cory's Shearwater)

46 cms in length. WIngspan 110 cms. Top of body grey, underparts whitish. Oblong bill slightly hooked at tip. A rare passage migrant.

2. Puffinus puffinus subsp. yelkouam (Manx Shearwater)

Very similar to 1 but smaller (35 cms) and darker, grey-black on top. Quite common to the seas surrounding Cyprus.

Hydrobatidae Family

Pelagic birds, like pigeons in outline. Feet webbed.

1. Hydrobates pelagicus (Storm Petrel)

Grey-black, with a white band at the base of the tail. 15 cms, in length. Legs and bill almost black. A rare, accidental visitor.

Black-necked Grebe.

Cory's Shearwater.

Manx Shearwater.

Dalmatian pelican.

Sulidae Family

Large sea-birds resembling pelicans, but with smaller, pouchless bills. Short, webbed feet.

1. Sula basana (Gannet)

Length 90 cms. White but for wing-tips which are black. Head tinged yellow. Grey bill. When immature grey all over. Nests in colonies on precipitous sea cliffs and feeds on fish. A West Mediterranean bird rarely appearing in the seas around Cyprus.

Pelecanidae Family

Large water-birds, generally white, short legs, webbed feet, and a long bill provided with a pouch in which they collect fish.

1. Pelecanus crispus (Dalmatian Pelican)

It measures from tail-tip to bill-tip 160-180 cms. Wingspan about 250 cms. White with a silver tinge on mantle; legs grey. Pouch orange. It dwells in lakes, lagoons and on coastal waters. Nests in wetlands. Passes through Cyprus on its migrations.

2. Pelecanus onocrotalus (White Pelican)

Similar to 1 but with lower half of wings showing black when in flight. A yellowish pouch. Yellowish-pink legs. A rare passage bird.

Phalacrocoracidae Family

Water birds, generally black in colour. Short legs with webbed feet. Elongated bill a little upturned at tip. Excellent swimmers, dive and often have only their heads out of water. Feed on fish.

1. Phalacrocorax carbo (Cormorant)

Black plumage, except for a white band round the base of its bill. Length 90 cms. It fishes in lakes, lagoons and other wetlands. Nests in trees. It appears in Cyprus in winter at rare and irregular intervals.

2. Phalacrocorax aristotelis (Shag)

Similar to 1 but all-black and smaller, about 76 cms. It fishes near the sea-coasts and nests on arid islets and coastal cliffs. A quite common resident species.

3. Phalacrocorax pygmaeus (Pygmy Cormorant)

Like 1 and 2 but only 48 cms. in length. It lives near fresh water and nests in reed-beds and trees. A rare passage migrant.

Otidae Family

Large three-toed land birds with strong legs. Toes and claws are short. The male larger than the female. Neck quite long.

1. Otis tarda (Great Bustard)

Chestnut, black-specked on upper parts; underparts white; head and throat pale grey. The male measures 102 cms and has two white feather tufts on base of bill. The female, (76cms), does not have the moustachial tufts of the male. A rare bird which in certain years comes as a winter visitor to Cyprus and Turkey.

2. Tetrax (Otis) tetrax (Little Bustard)

Like 1 but much smaller. about 43 cms. The male has a black neck and two black-and-

Cormorant

Shag

Great Bustard

Houbara Bustard

white bands on breast. The female is grey-beige with black specks. Formerly it came regularly to Cyprus in winter. At present, however, these visits have become exceptionally rare.

3. Chlamydotis undulata - subsp. macqueenii (Houbara Bustard)

Like 1 but smaller, 64 cms. It has two rows of black feathers at the two sides of the neck, and green legs. An African bird that only occasionally appears in Cyprus after long intervals.

Haematopodidae Family

These birds have a rather thick body, short tail, long bill, short neck and strong legs with the anterior toe very small. In appearance they look like woodcocks.

1. Haematopus ostralegus (Oystercatcher)

Length 43 cms. Bill and legs reddish. Upper parts of body black, and belly white. A bird of the coastal zone where it feeds on different crustaceans. Not very frequent appearances as a passage migrant, especially in spring.

Recurvirostridae Family

Birds with long legs, and bill long and thin, occasionally slightly curved. They reside in marshes.

1. Himantopus himantopus (Black-winged Stilt)

It is characterised by its very long and slim legs which are reddish. Bill dark-grey, slender and straight. Wings and back almost black. The rest of the body is white with a little grey on the crown of the head. Length 38 cms. As a spring passage migrant common. Small populations remain and breed in Cyprus.

2. Recurvirostra avosetta (Avocet)

A very characteristic bird with its black and white body and upturned bill. Its legs are grey but not so long as the Black-winged Stilt's. Length 43 cms. Not a very usual passage species.

Burhinidae Family

Ground birds of open spaces and deserts. Medium-sized bill. Strong legs, with only 3 toes on feet. Short tail. Eyes large and lively.

1. Burhinus oedicnemus - subsp. saharae (Stone Curlew)

A fairly large bird, 41 cms in length. General colouring like that of sand with darker specks. Yellowish legs, bill also yellowish with black tip. A rare bird which stays in Cyprus and breeds in bare localities, maquis, and wastelands.

Glareolidae Family

Birds with slender legs, usually swallow-tailed, long wings and small bill. Usually found near marshes and wetlands.

1. Glareola pratincola (Pratincole)

Grey-brown on head and upper parts, and pale beige on underparts, whitish at anterior part of belly. Wings reddish underneath. Swallow-tailed, black. 25cms. in length. A passage migrant.

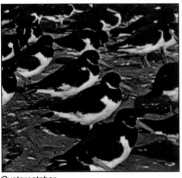
Oystercatcher.

Black-winged Stilt.

Avocet.

Stone Curlew.

2. Glareola nordmanni (Black-winged Pratincole)

Very like 1 but wings black underneath. 25cms in length. A rare bird of passage.

3. Cursorius cursor (Cream-coloured Courser)

Like two former species but bill longer and slightly curved. Beige-coloured tail very short, not forked. 2 bars, one black and one white over each eye. Wings white on underside, and black and beige on top. A bird found in solitary localities. Very few such birds have been observed as passage migrants.

Charadriidae Family

Wetland birds, bill short and slender, tail short, legs slender and of medium length, three-toed feet.

1. Vanellus vanellus (Lapwing)

A very pretty bird. A metallic green on upper part and white underneath. Breast and tail black. Nape and head white. A black crest and raised ribbonlike feathers. Reddish legs. Length 30 cms. A common winter visitor, mainly in the meadows of the central plain.

2. Vanellus (Chettusia) leucurus (White-tailed Plover)

In appearance like 1 but without the crest; body uniform beige with black on tip-end of wings. Yellowish legs longer, 28 cms. Rare accidental visits during its migrations. It winters in North East Africa and in summer it heads for the Middle East and Central Asia.

3. Vanellus (Hoplopterus) spinosus (Spur-winged Plover)

Similar to 1 but crestless. Mantle grey, head black and white, breast and throat black, and belly white. Legs grey. Length 27 cms. Sufficiently common as a passage migrant. It rarely remains to breed in Cyprus.

4. Pluvialis squatarola (Grey Plover)

Similar to Lapwing in appearance. Underparts black. Upper parts pale grey with dense black specks. Crown of head grey with black specks, flanks white and underparts black. Legs and bill grey. 28 cms in length. A rather rare passage bird and winter visitor.

5. Pluvialis apricaria (Golden Plover)

Very like 4 but on top golden with black specks. 28 cms in length. Quite a common winter visitor.

6. Charadrius hiaticula (Ringed Plover)

Upper parts grey-beige, underparts white. A black breastband. A black bar on eyes and a white spot on forehead. Black tail. Length 19 cms. Quite a common bird of passage.

7. Charadrius dubius - ssp. curonicus (Little Ringed Plover)

Very like 6 but smaller (15 cms) tail not black but same colour as mantle. A common passage migrant.

8. Charadrius alexandrinus (Kentish Plover)

Similar to the two former species but pale in colour. Distinguished by the two black spots situated behind the eye, and another two on each side of its throat. It has also a black spot

Collared Pratincole

Lapwing

Golden Plover

Ringed Plover

on its head. Length 16 cms. Quite common as a passage bird. There is, however, a small number of birds which remain and breed in Cyprus.

9. Charadrius leschenaultii (Greater Sand Plover)

Like the 3 previous species but larger, about 25 cms. Distinguishable by the light brown ring round its neck, and the black band on forehead which continues down to the sides right behind the eyes. A not very common passage bird.

10. Charadrius (Eudromias) morinellus (Dotterel)

Similar in appearance to the foregoing but darker coloured. Wings grey-brown, belly brown, mantle and throat grey. Head almost black on crown, with a white and black band at the height of the eyes. 22 cms long. A rare and accidental bird of passage.

Scolopacidae Family

Birds with a slender bill, medium-length or long, seldom slightly down-curving. Legs either short or medium. Tail short. They live in lowland meadows, in shallow marshes, or in wetlands in general.

1. Scolopax rusticola (Woodcock)

A short, thick body with a large head and a long bill. Short sturdy legs. Underparts beige with dark stripes, upperparts darker with black specks. Length 34 cms. Usually a common winter visitor in the mountain glades.

2. Gallinago media (Great Snipe)

Like 1 but smaller (28 cms). Dark grey legs. Smaller head. A sporadically appearing bird of passage.

3. Gallinago Gallinago (Snipe)

Like 1 and 2 but smaller (27cms) and with a longer bill. Belly whitish. Small flocks pass over Cyprus as birds of passage.

4. Limosa limosa (Black-tailed Godwit)

Like a snipe but breast brown and bill slightly upturned. In winter it turns a pale grey. Tail black-tipped. Length 41 cms. Not a very common bird of passage.

5. Limosa lapponica (Bar-tailed Godwit)

Almost like 4 but redder. Tail sports black and white lengthwise stripes. In winter the underparts turn almost white. Length 38 cms. A very rare passage migrant.

6. Calidris canutus (Knot)

Like 4 and 5 in colour but smaller (25 cms), with a straight and relatively short bill. Very rare passage bird.

7. Calidris ferruginea (Curlew Sandpiper)

The whole body reddish-brown in summer and grey in winter. Bill very slightly down-curved. Length 19 cms. A passage migrant.

8. Calidris alpina (Dunlin)

Similar to 7 but all-over beige-grey with black specks and black belly. In winter more

Woodcock.

Great Snipe.

Knot.

Sanderling.

uniform in colour - grey. Length 17-19 cms. A passage migrant and winter visitor.

9. Calidris alba (Sanderling)

In summer grey with dark specks and belly almost white. In winter colours paler, belly snow-white. Bill rather short and straight. Length 20 cms. A rare bird of passage.

10. Calidris temminckii (Temminck's Stint)

Similar to 9 but smaller (14 cms), and colouring a little darker. A rare passage bird˙

11. Calidris minuta (Little Stint)

Like 9 and 10 but still smaller (13 cms). A very common passage bird.

12. Philomachus pugnax (Ruff)

Like a Calidris. Grey plumage with dark specks. In the male the breast is all one colour. In winter grey, in summer the male sports a neckband and crest of bushy feathers useful in sexual displays; colours brighter. The neckband differs from individual to individual, from black to brown, to grey, and to white. Length 23 cms. A very common bird of passage.

13. Numenius phaeopus (Wimbrel)

Like a Calidris but bill long and down-curved. Grey with dark specks. Belly almost white. Length 41 cms. A rare passage bird.

14. Numenius tenuirostris (Slender-billed Curlew)

Very like 13 but more slender and longer. Length 41 cms. An occasional accidental visitor.

15. Numenius arquata (Curlew)

Like 13 and 14 but larger (53-58 cms) and with a longer bill. A passage bird and winter visitor.

16. Tringa erythropus (Spotted Redshank)

In summer this bird is black with white flecks. In winter dark grey on upper parts and pale grey on underparts. Bill straight and of medium length. Bill and legs reddish. Length 31 cms. Not a very common bird of passage.

17. Tringa nebularia (Greenshank)

Like 16 in winter but legs grey-green. Length 30 cms. A common passage bird.

18. Tringa totanus (Redshank)

Grey with dark flecks. Belly practically white. Length 28 cms. Legs red. A winter visitor.

19. Tringa stagnatilis (March Sandpiper)

Similar to 18 but smaller (23 cms). Specks brighter. Legs grey-green. Common as a bird of passage.

20. Tringa ochropus (Green Sandpiper)

Upper parts grey-black and light grey on underparts with black stripes across

Wimbrel

Spotted Redshank (Winter)

Greenshank

Wood Sandpiper

breast. Legs and bill grey-black. Length 23 cms. A common passage bird.

21. Tringa glareola (Wood Sandpiper)

Like 20 but only 20 cms in length. Colours paler and legs yellowish. Very common as a passage migrant.

22. Actitis (Tringa) hypoleucos (Common Sandpiper)

Mantle grey, belly white, head grey, breast grey with darker bars. Legs and bill shorter than those of the other sandpipers. Length 20 cms. A common bird of passage.

57

23. Xenus (tringa) cinereus (Terek Sandpiper)

Grey on top, almost white underneath. Legs and bill yellowish. Bill quite long, slightly up-curved. Length 23 cms. Occasionally appears in Cyprus in small numbers when migrating.

24. Arenaria interpes (Turnstone)

A strange bird with a short neck, small reddish legs, and upturned short bill. Upper parts grey-brown, underparts white. Wing and tail tips black. Head and breast patterned black and white. 23 cms in length. A rare passage visitor.

25. Phalaropus lobatus (Red-necked Phalarope)

Grey above, white below. Reddish spot on throat. In the female this spot is less bright, and in winter it disappears in both sexes. Legs and bill blackish. Legs, on the whole, long and slender. This bird is a shallow water wader and also a swimmer. A rare passage bird.

26. Limicola falcinelus (Broad-billed Sandpiper)

Grey-brown with darker specks. The belly a pale beige. Short legs. Bill quite long and straight except for the tip where it curves slightly downwards. Mostly a rare bird of passage.

27. Lymnocryptes minimus (Jack Snipe)

It looks like a small woodcock. Its length is 19 cms. Its belly almost white. Rather a rare bird of passage.

Stercorariidae Family

Birds like gulls but dark-coloured. Tail is wedge-shaped and has two slender and long feathers at the tip. They are pelagic birds which go to the shores of North Europe in summer to breed. They feed on the chicks of other sea-birds or they steal the food from the mouths of other birds.

1. Stercorarius parasiticus (Arctic Skua)

A grey-black bird with a black crown. Breast and neck grey. There are, however, individuals with a white breast and throat. Length 46 cms. An Altantic Ocean bird which enters the Mediterranean area in restricted numbers. In Cyprus it appears on rare occasions as a passage migrant.

Laridae Family

Sea or lake birds. They fly over the water and feed on fish. Excellent swimmers. Feet

Common Sandpiper.

Turnstone.

Herring Gull.

Audouin's Gull.

webbed. Nest on sea-cliffs. Often fly over land as well, especially in winter, feeding on rubbish, carcasses, or anything else they find.

1. Larus argentatus - subsp. michaelis (Herring Gull)

White on head, neck and underparts. Grey on top. Wings grey with black tips. Bill yellow. Legs greyish-pink. Tail white. Length 56-66 cms. A common Cyprus resident.

2. Larus fuscus (Lesser Black-beaked Gull)

Like 1 but the top part of body grey-black and legs yellow. Length 53-56 cms. A common passage migrant.

3. Larus audouinii (Audouin's Gull)

Like 1 but legs a greyish-black, and reddish bill with a black band and yellow tip. 50 cms. long. A rare bird that resides and multiplies on the rocky islets round Cyprus.

4. Larus canus (Common Gull)

Very like 1 but smaller (41cms). Legs and bill yellow. A rare winter visitor.

5. Larus genei (Slender-billed Gull)

Like 1 but only 43 cms. in length. Slender bill. Legs and bill reddish. A common passage migrant.

6. Larus marinus (Great Black-backed Gull)

In colour very like Lesser Black-backed Gull, but in size larger (64-79 cms). Another difference is the colour of the legs that are pink. An Atlantic Ocean bird that rarely makes its way into the Mediterranean area. Its appearances in Cyprus are occasional.

7. Larus ichthyaetus (Great Black-headed Gull)

A large gull 66 cms. On top grey and white below. Wings black-tipped. Beak black. Bill yellow and at tip red and black. Yellow legs. Resides in river deltas, lakes, and inland seas such as the Caspian Sea. Its accidental appearance in Cyprus has been observed only once.

8. Larus melanocephalus (Mediterranean Gull)

Like 7 but much smaller - 39 cms. Legs red, and wings white-tipped. In older times a common bird of passage and winter visitor. Last seen in Cyprus in 1978.

9. Larus ridibundus (Black-headed Gull)

Similar to 7 but only 35-38 cms in length. Legs reddish. Head brownish-black. A common winter visitor.

10. Larus minutus (Little Gull)

The smallest of the black-headed gulls, measuring 28 cms. Legs and bill reddish. Wings grey above and grey-black beneath. A not very common winter visitor.

11. Rissa tridactyla (Kittiwake)

Very similar in size and colours to the Common Gull, only that the legs are blackish.

Slender-billed Gull

Mediterraneam Gull

Kittiwake

Common Tern

An Atlantic Ocean and West Mediterranean bird that appears in Cyprus only occasionally.

Sternidae Family

Birds resembling Gulls but with a more pointed bill and swallow-tailed. Reside in wetlands and usually nest on the ground.

1. Hydroprogne tschegrava (Caspian Tern)

Light grey on upper parts and white on underparts. A crest of black feathers on crown

61

of head. Strong, red bill. Black legs. White tail. Length 53 cms. A rare passage migrant.

2. Sterna sandvicensis (Sandwich Tern)

Like 1 but smaller - 41 cms. Slender bill, black and yellow at tip. Accidental winter visitor.

3. Sterna hirundo (Common Tern)

Like 1 and 2 but smaller (35 cms). The black feathers on head do not form a crest. Legs red. A black-tipped red bill. A common passage bird. In former times a few pairs had been noted nesting on Cyprus.

4. Sterna Paradisaea (Arctic Tern)

Almost identical with former but breast and belly a light grey and bill entirely red. A rare, accidental visitor.

5. Sterna albifrons (Little Tern)

Almost the same as 3 and 4 but smaller (24 cms), legs and bill yellow. A passage migrant which occasionally nests on Cyprus in small numbers.

6. Chlidonias niger (Black Tern)

Similar in silhouette to the other terns, but wings grey-black and rest of body black. Both bill and legs black. In winter the colour is paler. Length 24 cms. Quite a common bird of passage.

7. Chlidonias Leucopterus (White-winged Black Tern)

Like 6 but wings a light grey, bill and legs red. In winter grey on top and almost white underneath. A common passage bird.

8. Chlidonias hybrida (Whiskered Tern)

Like 6 but colours in general paler, wings and mantle grey. Breast grey-black. Head with a black crown and whitish at sides. Legs and bill red. In winter nearly white. A rare passage migrant.

9. Gelochelidon nilotica (Gull-billed Tern)

Similar to other terns. On top light grey and white over rest of body. The crown of the head black and crestless. Strong black bill. Legs black. Not a very common bird of passage.

Pteroclididae Family

The appearance of the birds of this family is something between a pigeon's and a

Black tern.

Black-bellied Sandgrouse.

Gull-billed Tern.

Rock Dove.

partridge's. The all-over colour is sandy, but often impressively mottled. They live in deserts and on barren plains.

1. Pterocles orientalis (Black-bellied Sandgrouse)

The male is sand-coloured on the upper part of the body. Belly black. Breast and throat grey with a narrow black band on breast. Legs and feet, except for toes, covered in grey feathers. The female is similar but the upper parts are covered with dense black bars and specks. Length 34 cms. One of the rarest and prettiest birds of Cyprus. A few dozen can still be found on the Central Plain where they reside permanently. In former times they were far more numerous.

2. Pterocles alchata-ssp. caudacutus (Pin-tailed Sandgrouse)

The most handsome species of the Pterocles genus. Underparts white, upper parts a pale green. A wide breast with a reddish neckband. The head a citrus green. The tail ends in two slender long feathers. The female is sand-coloured on top with black specks and bars. It is a species belonging to N. Africa, Spain, and W. Asia. Said to have resided in Cyprus in days gone by. However, it is not certain whether it was a permanent resident of the island or a migrant. Today, in any case, it appears to have disappeared.

Columbidae Family

The species of this family look more or less like the domestic dove. They nest on rocks or on trees and feed on seeds.

1. Columba livia (Rock Dove)

A general grey. At the tip of the tail a black band. Two black bands on wings. Throat a metallic greenish-purple. At the base of tail a white spot. 33 cms. in length. This species is the ancestor of the domesticated pigeon. It nests on precipitous sea-cliffs or on the islets around Cyprus. It is also found in the mountains in ravines and gorges. It is quite a common permanent Cyprus resident.

2. Columba oenas (Stock Dove)

Very like 1 but without the bands on the wings and the white spot base of the tail. Length 33 cms. Nests in trees. Not a very frequent winter visitor.

3. Columba palumbus (Woodpigeon)

Similar to the former two but larger (41 cms). Has a white band on each wing and a white spot on either side of the neck. Nests in the dense mountain forests on both mountain ranges. Quite a common permanent resident.

4. Streptopelia decaocto (Collared Dove)

Similar to a Rock Dove but smaller, only 32 cms. A greyish-fawn, mantle darker. Legs reddish. A black band at the base of neck. Nests in trees, especially in town parks. A permanent Cyprus resident.

5. Streptopelia turtur (Turtle Dove)

Like 4 but smaller (27 cms). Back light brown with black specks. Tail black with white tip. A common bird of passage. Small populations remain and bread in localities of scattered trees.

6. Streptopelia senegalensis (Palm Dove)

Similar to 5 but smaller (25 cms). Back and head a brownish-red. Wings grey-black. Belly beige. Tail black white-edged. A collar of black spots and bars on breast. A rare accidental visitor.

Stock Dove

Collared Dove

Woodpigeon

Cuckoo

Cuculidae Family

Birds with a long slender and slightly curved bill. They are usually parasitic birds laying their eggs in the nests of other birds.

1. Cuculus canorus (Cuckoo)

Grey, tail blackish similar to wing-tips. White belly densely striped in darker colours. There are individuals all over brown with black specks (Brown phase). 33 cms in length. A passage migrant. It is probable that some individuals stay and breed on the Troodos Range.

2. Clamator glandarius (Great Spotted Cuckoo)

Like 1 but larger (39 cms) with throat, breast and belly almost white. Small crest on head. A passage migrant which in passing through the island often lays its eggs in magpie (pica pica) nests, or in those of Hooded Crows (Corvus corone).

3. Chrysococcyx caprius (Didric Cuckoo)

General colour a metallic green except on belly which is yellow. Length 18-20 cms. An African species that only occasionally visits Cyprus. It was first noted there in 1982. That is also the first time the species was noted in the whole of the Palaioarctic Zone (Europe-Asia).

Apodidae Family

Insectivores, in appearance similar to swallows. Very small bill. Legs small and slender. Long, narrow, sturdy wings.

1. Apus melba (Alpine Swift)

Colouring generally grey to brown. Throat and belly white. Breast grey. Swallow-tailed but only slightly forked. 22 cms. Nests in mountain precipices. Known in Cyprus only as a common bird of passage.

2. Apus pallidus (Pallid Swift)

Like 1 but all one colour save for throat which is slightly paler. Length 16,5 cms. It is a common enough species which comes to Cyprus in spring and breeds there.

3. Apus apus (Swift)

Similar to 1 but one-coloured, darker than 2, almost black. 16,5 cms long. A common summer visitor which breeds in Cyprus. Resides in towns and villages.

Alcedinidae Family

Birds with long, pointed bills, short legs. Tail either short or medium length. Brightly coloured. Usually feed on fish which they catch with their bills as they fly over the surface of the water in wetlands.

1. Alcedo atthis (Kingfisher)

An impressively coloured bird. Red beneath and blue above. A red bar over the eyes. White throat. Short tail. Length 16,5 cms. Both a passage bird and a winter visitor.

2. Halcyon smyrnensis (White-breasted or Smyrna Kingfisher)

Similar to 1 but larger (27 cms), tail longer. Head and belly greyish-red. Throat and breast white. A W. Asian bird occasionally appearing in Cyprus.

Didric Cuckoo

Pallid Swift

Swift

Kingfisher

3. Ceryle rudis (Pied Kingfisher)

Like 1 but grey-black on top and white beneath. On breast a band of 2 black bars on male and one on female. In the female the band is disrupted in the centre. Bill and legs black. Length 25 cms. A West Asian bird that appears in Cyprus as a rare winter visitor.

Meropidae Family

Insectivores. Brilliant colours. Short legs. Bill slender, quite long, and a little down-curved. Medium-length tail with two long, slender, pointed feathers at tip.

1. Merops apiaster (Bee-eater)

Belly and breast blue. Crown of head and back reddish-orange. Tail greenish. Throat yellow.

67

A black band across eyes and on breast. Length 28 cms. Common as a bird of passage, especially in spring. Small populations stay and breed on Cyprus.

2. Merops superciliosus-subsp. persicus (Blue-cheeked Bee-eater)

Similar to 1 but larger (31 cms) and colours more greenish. The two tail feathers are much longer than those of 1. Very few such birds pass through Cyprus as passage migrants.

Coraciidae Family

Large, many-coloured birds that feed on small animals. Tail quite long. Bill rather short and strong. Legs short.

1. Coracias garrulus (Roller)

Head and underparts blue. Back copper-coloured. Wings and tail two-coloured: blue and black. Length 31 cms. A common bird of passage. Small flocks stay and breed on Cyprus.

Upupidae Family

Birds with a beautiful crest of feathers on head, and a long, slender, pointed bill which is a little curved. They feed on insects they find in manure, among rotten leaves or in rubbish.

1. Upupa epops (Hoopoe)

A lovely bird with head, breast and belly brown. Back, wings and tail two-coloured with black and white bands. Crest feathers brown with black tips. A common bird of passage. Length 28 cms. A few pairs remain in summer and breed in the mountain forests of Cyprus.

Picidae Family

Insectivores. Most of the species peck at the rotten trees with their bills to bring out the insects concealed in them. They have the ability both to stand and climb vertically on the tree trunks with two toes pointing backwards and two forwards.

1. Jynx torquilla (Wryneck)

This is the smallest member of the family. Because of its small size it is unable to pierce the wood. Therefore it feeds on the insects it finds on the tree trunks, mainly ants. All over colour grey-beige with darker specks. Length 16,5 cms. A common passage bird. A few stay and winter in Cyprus.

Alaudidae Family

Small or medium-sized birds, crested or not. Feet suitable for walking on the ground with the

White-breasted or Smyrna Kingfisher

Bee-eater

Blue-cheeked Bee-eater

Hoopoe

hind toe and claw usually longer than the others. Short conical bill, on rare occasions longer and slightly down-curved.

1. Melanocorhypha calandra (Calandra Lark)

Grey with dark specks except for the belly and throat which are white. A black collar on breast. Crestless head. The hind claw very long. Length 19 cms. Well-known by its loud melodious song. Quite large numbers of these birds reside permanently in Cyprus.

2. Melanocorhypha bimaculata (Bimaculated Lark)

Like 1 but grey-brown on top and fawn underneath. The black collar on breast much narrower, breaking off in the centre. Length 16,5 cms. An Asian species, appearing in Cyprus, rarely, as an accidental visitor.

3. Calandrella brachydactyla (cinerea) (Short-toed Lark)

Similar to the Calandra Lark but smaller (14 cms) and without a collar on the breast. The hind claw not very long. A common summer visitor which remains and breeds in Cyprus. Large flocks cross Cyprus as birds of passage.

4. Calandrella rufescens (Lesser Short-toed Lark)

Similar to 3 but the upperparts more speckled. Length 14 cms. Rare bird of passage.

5. Ammomanes desertii - (Desert Lark)

It differs for the other larks, being practically a uniform sand-colour, lighter on the underparts. Only the tips of the wings are black. A North African and West Asian desert bird, and a rarely observed accidental visitor in Cyprus.

6. Galerida cristata-subsp. caucasica (Crested Lark)

Similar to the Calandra Lark in colour, but smaller (17 cms), without black on breast, but with a crest. Hind claw long. A very common resident species.

7. Lullula arborea-subsp. pallida (Wood Lark)

Very like the Crested Lark but smaller (15 cms), and with a much smaller crest, just noticeable. A common resident species.

8. Alauda arvensis-subsp. cantarella (Skylark)

Very similar to 6 and 7 but larger (18 cms). Its crest is smaller than the Crested Lark's. A very common winter visitor.

Hirundidae Family

Birds with long wings, short legs, small bills, tail either forked or not. They feed on insects which they catch in flight.

1. Hirundo rustica (Swallow)

Black on top, white underneath. Throat brownish-red. Deeply forked tail with elongated outer feathers. 19 cms in length. Nests in stables, on verandas, balconies, under eaves etc. A common summer visitor.

2. Hirundo daurica-subsp. rufula (Red-rumped Swallow)

Similar to 1 but elongated outer tail feathers slightly shorter. The white on the belly reaches the

Bimaculated Lark

Crested Lark

Swallow

Sand Martin

throat, the nape and the back part of the mantle, taking on a brownish hue. Length 18 cms. It builds its nest under projecting cliffs, on steep slopes and in gorges. A common summer visitor.

3. Delichon urbica (House Martin)

Like 1 but smaller-sized (12,5 cms), with very short outer tail feathers. Underparts and anterior of back snow-white. Builds nest under the eaves of houses and on cliffs in gorges. A common summer visitor.

4. Riparia riparia (Sand Martin)

Like 3 but grey on top not black. On breast a grey band. Length 12 cms. Builds its nest on sea-cliff faces and on banks. A common passage bird.

5. Ptyonoprogne (Hirundo) rupestris (Crag Martin)

Upper parts grey, very light grey-beige underparts. Tail not forked. Length 14 cms. Builds nest on crags in gorges. Quite common as a bird of passage. Small flocks stay on in Cyprus the whole year round and breed there.

Motocilidae Family

Small to medium-sized birds with a slender and pointed bill. Tail medium to long, and legs slender.

1. Anthus novaeseelandiae-subsp. richardii (Richard's Pipit)

Underparts a fawnish-white and grey-brown on upper parts. Black specks on breast. Hind claws long. Length 18 cms. One of the largest species of the family. It appears rarely in Cyprus as a bird of passage.

2. Anthus campestris (Tawny Pipit)

Grey, much lighter on belly, with no specks on breast, length 16.5 cms. Quite common as a bird of passage.

3. Anthus similis (Long-billed Pipit)

Very like 2 but paler in general, and bill a little longer. Length 19 cms. A West Asia and Middle East bird appearing in Cyprus but rarely, as an accidental visitor.

4. Anthus pratensis (Meadow Pipit)

Similar to 1 but greyer and smaller (14.5 cms), and with thicker and darker specks on breast. A very common winter visitor.

5. Anthus trivialis (Tree Pipit)

Resembles 4 a lot but is just a little larger (15 cms), colour darker fawn. On the breast thick dark specks.

6. Anthus cervinus (Red-throated Pipit)

Very nearly white on underparts and grey on top. The breast is adorned with thick rows of black specks which in summer almost disappear, giving place to a reddish hue. The hind claw is long. Length 14.5 cms. A common passage bird.

7. Anthus spinoletta (Water Pipit)

General colouring dark grey. Legs and bill blackish. Hind claw not very long. On breast darker specks, not very vivid, which disappear completely in summer. Length 16.5 cms. A common enough passage bird.

Crag Martin

Tawny Pipit

Meadow Pipit

Grey Wagtail

8. Motacilla flava (Yellow Wagtail)

A relatively small bird with a long tail. The upper parts of the body are grey, the underparts golden-yellow. Blackish tail. Legs and bill blackish too. Length 16.5 cms. In winter the yellow colour of belly and breast fades and becomes almost beige. A common passage bird.

9. Motacilla cinerea (Grey Wagtail)

Similar in size and colours to 8 but tail is longer, almost as long as body, and the throat is usually black in the male, nearly white in the female. Length 18 cms. Light-coloured legs. It appears in Cyprus both as a bird of passage and as a winter migrant.

10. Motacilla citreola (Citrine Wagtail)

Similar to 8 but besides having its underparts yellow its head is yellow too. Length 16.5 cms. An Asiatic species which makes rare and accidental appearances in Cyprus.

11. Motacilla alba (White Wagtail)

Like 8 but with white underparts. Head white with a black cap. Breast and throat black. A common passage bird and winter visitor. Length 18 cms. Some pairs stay and breed in Cyprus.

Bombycillidae Family

Pretty woodland birds. Bill short and rather thick. Legs rather short. There is often a crest on the head.

1. Bombycilla garrulus (Waxwing)

General colour brown-grey. Throat black. Tail blue with a yellow tip. Wings many-coloured, with black, yellow, white, and blue feathers. Head bears a crest which the bird can raise at will. Length 18 cms. A rare winter visitor.

Cinclidae Family

Birds with a short tail, short feathers and slender legs. They reside near running water diving into it to find their food.

1. Cinclus cinclus (Dipper)

Length 18 cms. General colouring dark grey. On belly a brownish hue, while breast and throat are white. In older times it resided permanently in Cyprus close to the mountain streams on the Troodos Range. Today it has disappeared.

Troglodytidae Family

Small birds with a short, plump body, a slender pointed bill, and a short tail which they raise upwards.

1. Troglodytes troglodytes-subsp. cypriotes (Cypriot Wren)

Back brown, underparts beige with darker specks and stripes towards rump. Length 9.5 cms. A common permanent resident in Cyprus, especially on the Troodos Range.

White Wagtail

Dunnock

Blackbird

Ring Ouzel

Prunelidae Family

Small birds with a slender pointed bill, medium-length tail, and slender legs. They live chiefly in the mountains.

1. Prunella modularis (Dunnock)

Head and underparts dark grey. Upper parts a greyish-brown. Length 14.5 cms. A winter visitor.

Turdidae Family

Small or medium-sized birds with a rather small and slender bill. Slender legs. Tail medium.

1. Turdus merula (Blackbird)

Male black, female dark grey. Legs grey. Bill yellow. Length 25 cms. A common winter visitor.

2. Turdus torquatus (Ring Ouzel)

Like 1 but there is a white band on the breast, and the bill is a greyish-yellow. Length 24 cms. Not very frequent appearances as a passage bird or winter visitor.

3. Turdus viscivorous (Mistle Thrush)

Similar to both former species in silhouette, but very different in colour. Top is dark grey-beige, underparts light beige with big dark specks. Bill grey. Length 27 cms. A winter visitor.

4. Turdus philomelos (Song Thrush)

Very like 3 but smaller (23 cms), and breast a light brown. A very common winter visitor.

5. Turdus iliacus (Redwing)

Like 3 and 4 but a smaller size (21 cms), darker on top and reddish on belly flanks. A winter visitor.

6. Turdus pilaris (Fieldfare)

Wings and back grey-brown. Head grey. Tail grey-black. Belly white. Breast and throat fawn with dark specks. Length 25.5 cms. A winter visitor.

7. Turdus naumanni (Dusky or Naumann's Thrush)

On top grey-brown. Underneath a pale pinkish-beige, darker brown on breast. Dark brown tail. Dark specks only on sides of throat. However, they often spread towards breast and flanks **(subsp. euonomus).** One bird caught in Cyprus had characteristics between those of the **subsp. naumanni** and those of the **subsp. euonomus.** A very rare accidental visitor.

8. Monticola solitarius (Blue Rock Thrush)

Similar to a blackbird but the male a blue-grey with the upper parts and tail darker. Bill and legs dark grey. The female is dark grey with lighter specks. Length 20 cms. A permanent resident of Cyprus, especially of the northern range.

9. Monticola saxatilis (Rock Thrush)

Like 8 but smaller (19 cms), with the breast and belly brown. The female like the female of 8 but of a lighter tone. A rare bird of passage, especially in spring.

10. Oenanthe hispanica-subsp. melanoleuca (Black-eared Wheatear)

General colour beige-white. Wings black. Long black oblong spots on either side of

Mistle Thrush

Redwing

Blue Rock Thrush

Rock Thrush

head. Legs and bill blackish. Tail black at tip, white at base. Back part of body nearly white. Female like male but the dark areas of body are brown instead of black. Length 14.5 cms.

11. Oenanthe oenathe (Common Wheatear)

Like 10 but the mantle and the crown of the head of the male are grey. Length 14.5 - 15 cms. Very common bird of passage, especially in spring.

12. Oenanthe deserti (Desert Wheatear)

Like 10 only the black on sides of head extends to the throat. Length 14.5 cms. A passage migrant. Rare.

13. Oenanthe cypriaca (Cyprus Pied Wheatear)

Similar to 10 but in the males the black extends from the wings to the back, and from the sides of the head to the throat. This is a Cyprus endemic which breeds in Cyprus, but in winter migrates to Ethiopia and S. Sudan. Formerly it was considered a form of Oenanthe pleschanka which lives in a more easterly direction, in West Asia.

14. Oenanthe finschii (Finsch's Wheatear)

The male similar to the former. The female grey on top and almost white below, throat and sides of head dark grey. Quite a common winter visitor.

15. Oenanthe leucopyga (White-crowned Black Wheatear)

The male is black except on back of head, anterior of belly and the outer tail feathers. In the female the general colour is a more washed-out black. The crown of the head is also black. Length 13.5 cms. A North Africa bird appearing in Cyprus only as an accidental and occasional visitor.

16. Oenanthe monacha (Hooded Wheatear)

Similar to 15 but besides white tail, and white back of head, the male's belly is white as well. The female is grey-beige. Length 17 cms. A Middle East and South West Asia bird, noted in Cyprus as an accidental and rare visitor.

17. Oenanthe isabellina (Isabelline Wheatear)

The only species where the male and female have no essential differences. General colour beige, darker on wings. The tip of tail black. Length 16.9 cms. A common passage bird.

18. Saxicola torquata-subsp. rubicola (Stonechat)

Black except for belly and breast which are reddish. White spots on throat, wings, and at the base of tail. Female similar but with upper parts greyish-brown instead of black. Length 12.5 cms. Very common as a winter visitor.

19. Saxicola rubetra (Whinchat)

Similar to 18 but back, head, and tail greyish-brown with dark flecks. Belly, breast, and throat reddish-beige. Wings a brownish-black. The female has the same colours but paler. Length 12.5 cms. A common passage migrant.

20. Phoenicurus ochrurus-subsp. gibraltariensis (Black Redstart)

In general, grey with a brown tail. Male a greyish-black. Female paler. Length 14 cms. A common winter visitor.

Common Wheatear

Cyprus Pied Wheatear

Whinchat

Black Redstart

21. Phoenicurus phoenicurus (Redstart)

Like 20 but belly and breast brown, and a white spot on forehead. Female much lighter in colour and without the spot on forehead. Length 14 cms. A common bird of passage. In Cyprus two subspecies may be observed: the local **P. p. phoenicurus,** and the subspecies **samamisicus** in which the males have a white spot on the wings.

22. Irania gutturalis (White-throated Robin)

Very similar to 21 but it has a black tail and white throat. The colours in the females are duller. Length 16.5 cms. A rare accidental visitor from West Asia.

23. Tarsiger cyanurus (Red-flanked Bluetail)

Head, tail and mantle dark blue. Throat white. Underparts light grey, and flanks reddish. The male's blue parts are grey in the female. It is a species that migrates in summer from Asia to Northern Europe. It has been observed in Cyprus only once - in 1957 - as an accidental visitor.

24. Luscinia megarhynchos (Nightingale)

Over-all colour grey-fawn with tail brownish. Length 16.5 cms. A usual summer visitor. It resides mainly in the forests, and the mountain ravines.

25. Luscinia luscinia (Thrush Nightingale)

Nearly identical with 24 but slightly darker on top, and tail a greyish-brown. Very light specks on breast. A common passage bird.

26. Luscinia svecica (Bluethroat)

Similar to the two former species but the throat is blue, ending in a three-coloured band - black, white and red. The base of tail brown. Length 14 cms. A passage migrant. Flocks of the **subsp. svecica,** with the whole of the throat blue, have been observed, have flocks of the **subsp. cyanecula** which have a white spot right in the middle of the blue.

27. Erithacus rubecula (Robin)

Mantle grey-brown. Belly white. Breast, throat and under the head a brownish-red. Length 14 cms. A common winter visitor.

28. Cercotrichas galactotes-subsp. syriacus (Rufous Bush Chat)

Like the Nightingale, but the tail which it often raises gracefully is brown, longer, and wedge-shaped at tip. Wings and back grey-brown. Length 15 cms. Not a very common passage bird.

Sylviidae Family

Small insectivores with a slender bill.

1. Sylvia hortensis (Orphean Warbler)

Upper parts dark grey, underparts very light. Head black except for throat that is light grey. Blackish tail. Female's head dark grey. Legs blackish. Length 15 cms. Common passage bird.

White-throated Robin

Nightingale

Robin

Sardinian Warbler

2. Sylvia atricapilla (Blackcap)

Like 1 but only crown of head black. In the female the crown is brown. Length 14 cms.
Common both as passage bird and as winter visitor.

3. Sylvia melanocephala (Sardinian Warbler)

Like 1 but smaller (13.5 cms), back dark grey but somewhat more reddish. Legs slightly
lighter in colour. A common winter visitor.

4. Sylvia rueppelli (Rüppell's Warbler)

Like 1 but male sports a black throat and breast. 14 cms in length. A bird of passage.

5. Sylvia conspicillata (Spectacled Warbler)

Like 1 but wings a grey-brown and belly fawn. Head grey-black. Length 12.5 cms. A common permanent Cyprus resident.

6. Sylvia candillans (Subalpine Warbler)

Male dark grey on top, female lighter. Male underparts beige-brown, female's beige. A characteristic white line on both sides of head starting at the bill and looking like a moustache. Length 12 cms. Bird of passage. Appears mostly in spring.

7. Sylvia melanothorax (Cyprus Warbler)

Resembles the Sardinian Warbler (Sylvia melanocephala. But the throat, breast, and belly-flanks have lovely dark.flecks which in the female are fewer and lighter-coloured. Length 13.5 cms. A permanent Cyprus resident. It is a rare endemic species of Cyprus, Palestine, and the Lebanon.

8. Sylvia communis (Whitethroat)

Male and female almost identical. Head and breast grey. Wings and tail grey-brown. Underparts very light grey-beige. Head grey-black. Length 12.5 cms. A common bird of passage.

9. Sylvia borin (Garden Warbler)

Like 8 but on top grey, and beneath very pale grey. Length 14 cms. Quite a common bird of passage.

10. Sylvia nisoria (Barred Warbler)

Looks like the Cyprus Warbler with the characteristic specks on the underparts, but its colours are in general much paler. Length 15 cms. A rare bird of passage.

11. Sylvia curruca (Lesser Whitethroat)

On top grey and underneath nearly white. Sides of head nearly black. Length 13.5 cms. A common bird of passage.

12. Sylvia nana (Desert Warbler)

On top grey, underneath almost white. Bill and legs light-coloured. Length 11.5 cms. A West Asia and North Africa bird which in Cyprus has been noted only as an accidental visitor.

13. Hippolais icterina (Icterine Warbler)

Olive-green on back and head, a pale yellowy-green on under-parts. Wings and tail dark olive-green. Over eye a characteristic yellow line like an eyebrow. Length 13.5 cms. A rare passage migrant.

Spectacled Warbler

Cyprus Warbler

Icterine Warbler

Great Reed Warbler

14. Hippolais pallida (Olivaceous Warbler)

Like 13 but the general colour tends to fawn. Length 13.5 cms. A very common summer visitor.

15. Hippolais olivetorum (Olive-tree Warbler)

Top of body grey. Underparts very light. Wings and tail grey-black. Length 15 cms. Not a very usual bird of passage.

16. Acrocephalus arundinaceus (Great Reed Warbler)

A wetland bird. Grey-brown upper parts, light grey-beige under parts. Tail tip rounded.

Length 19 cms. Quite a common passage bird. A few pairs stay on and breed in Cyprus.

17. Acrocephalus scirpaceus-subsp. fuscus (Reed Warbler)

Similar to 16. A wetlands bird, but smaller, 12.5 cms in length. Its colour is a little darker too. Quite a common summer visitor.

18. Acrocephalus palustris (March Warbler)

Almost identical with former, but back darker. A passage migrant. It passes through Cyprus more specifically in autumn.

19. Acrocephalus melanopogon (Moustached Warbler)

Fawn below, brown with dark specks above. Head fawn, dark brown on crown and sides. A light-coloured line over eyes. Length 13 cms. Not a very usual winter visitor.

20. Acrocephalus schoenobaenus (Sedge Warbler)

Very like 19 but slightly lighter-coloured. A bird of passage.

21. Locustella luscionioides (Savi's Warbler)

A marsh bird, dark brown on top and beige underneath. Rounded tail tip. Length 14 cms. Not a very usual passage migrant.

22. Locustella fluviatilis (River Warbler)

Almost the same as 21 but on breast and on flanks there are darker specks, but not very vivid. Length 13 cms. A very rare bird of passage.

23. Locustella naevia (Grasshopper Warbler)

Like 21 but smaller (13 cms) with dark specks on back and head. Has been noted in Cyprus only as an accidental visitor.

24. Cettia cetti (Cetti's Warbler)

Very similar to Savi's Waqrbler but darker, browny-black on top and tail wider. Length 14 cms. A bird of the wetlands. A permanent resident.

25. Cisticola jundicis (Fan-tailed Warbler)

General colouring fawn. Underparts monochrome. Upper body with dark specks. Tail wide. Seen from below one observes black and white dots around the edges. Length 10 cms. A marsh bird. A common permanent resident.

Sedge Warbler

Savi's Warbler

Fan-tailed Warbler

Dusky Warbler

26. Phylloscopus sibilatrix (Wood Warbler)

Upper part of body olive green. Belly almost white. Breast and throat a yellowy-green. Legs light-coloured. Length 12.5 cms. A common enough bird of passage.

27. Phylloscopus collybita (Chiffchaff)

Similar to 26 but, in gerenal, colours less green, shading more towards grey. Legs dark-coloured. Length 11 cms. Very common both as a migrant and as a winter visitor.

28. Phylloscopus trochilus (Willow Warbler)

Almost identical with the former. Legs light-coloured. Length 11 cms. Not a very common migrant. Flies over Cyprus chiefly in spring.

29. Phylloscopus inornatus (Yellow-browed Warbler)

A greyish-green on top. Belly practically white. Breast and throat a very pale greyish olive-green. Length 10 cms. An accidental visitor.

30. Phylloscopus bonelli-subsp. orientalis (Bonelli's Warbler-oriental forme)

Greyish-brown on top, greyish-olive-green towards tail and wings. Underneath buff. Legs blackish. Length 11.5 cms. A passage bird.

31. Phylloscopus fuscatus (Dusky Warbler)

Upper part dark brown. Underparts beige. Legs brownish-black. Length 11 cms. An Asiatic species observed in Cyprus only as a rare accidental visitor.

32. Regulus regulus (Goldcrest)

A small bird. Olive-green on top, grey below. Wings and tail shading towards black. A black line over eyes. Crown of head orange in males, yellow in females. Length 9 cms. A winter visitor.

33. Regulus ignicapilus (Firecrest)

Same as 32 but colours brighter, and two parallel black lines over eyes. A very rare visitor.

Muscicapidae Family

Small birds with a small slender bill, and slender legs. Feed on insects.

1. Ficedula hypoleuca (Pied Flycatcher)

The two sexes differ in colour. Male black above, snow-white below. White band on black wings. Female a greyish-brown instead of black on top, underneath a very pale grey, 13 cms in length. A bird of passage, largely in spring.

2. Ficedula albicolis (Collared Flycatcher)

Very similar in colour with 1 especially the hen. The male differs by having a white collar, and a large white spot on brow. Length 12.5 cms. A spring migrant.

3. Ficedula semitorquata (Semi-collared Flycatcher)

Characteristic intermediaries between the two former species. The white collar does not encircle the throat completely. The two end tail feathers are white. Not a very usual spring bird of passage.

Goldcrest

Pied Flycatcher

Red-breasted Flycatcher

Bearded Tit

4. Ficedula parva (Red-breasted Flycatcher)

Grey on top, beige underneath. In the male throat and breast orange-coloured. Length 11.5 cms. A very rare bird of passage.

5. Muscicapa striata - subsp. naumanni (Spotted Flycatcher)

A greyish-brown on top, pale grey underneath. Breast darkly mottled. Ditto crown of head. Length 14 cms. Quite common as a summer visitor, particularly in the mountain forests.

Timalidae Family

Very pretty, multicoloured birds. They look like Tits in outline but their tails are especially long.

1. Panurus biarmicus (Bearded Tit or Bearded Reedling)

Generally, a rosy-beige on upper parts and creamy on underparts. In males the all-over colouring is brighter. In addition, there are: a) a black downstroke fleck under each eye; b) a black spot on base of tail, and c) the head is somewhat greyish-blue. A rare winter visitor.

Paridae Family

Small insectivore birds, small-billed, tail medium to long.

1. Parus major - subsp. aphroditae (Cyprus Great Tit)

Back olive-green. Belly creamy-white. Wings grey. Tail greyish-black. Head black, except for cheeks which are white. Throat black extending in a narrow ribbon towards breast and belly. Length of body 14 cms. A permanent Cyprus resident. An endemic subspecies, differing from the typical form chiefly in the colour of the belly. In the typical form found in Asia and Europe the belly is yellow.

2. Parus ater - subsp. cypriotes (Cyprus Coal Tit)

Like 1 but smaller (11.5 cms). Breast and belly grey-brown. The black on throat does not extend towards breast and belly. A permanent resident. An endemic subspecies of Cyprus.

Tichodromadidae Family

Birds with medium-sized strong legs, a slender bill long and slightly downcurving. Short tail. Wings short too. They habitually walk vertically on the sheer sides of mountains and gorges.

1. Tichodroma muraria (Wallcreeper)

Back and crown of head grey. Tail black. Wings reddish at base and black at the edges. Belly, breast, and throat black. In winter the throat turns grey. Length 16.5 cms. A winter visitor.

Certhiidae Family

Birds similar in outline with the above, but tail longer with hard feathers, bill shorter. They strut up and down tree trunks feeding on insects.

1. Certhia brachydactyla - subsp. dorotheae (Cyprian Short-toed Treecreeper)

Top parts of body dark greyish-brown mottled with pale flecks. Underparts white. Length 12.5 cms. An endemic Cyprian form of the widely distributed C. brachydactyla species. A permanent resident of the Troodos Range forests.

Remizidae Family

This family is related to the Tits from which it differs in secondary and not distinctive characteristics.

Cyprus Great Tit

Cyprus Coal Tit

Wallcreeper

Golden Oriole

1. Remiz pendulinus (Penduline Tit)

Wings and back brown. Wings blackish at edges. Tail greyish-black. Head, back, throat, breast white. Belly beige. On head a black band in line with the eyes. On the whole a rare winter visitor.

Oriolidae Family

Medium-sized birds, usually with bright plumage. Bill slender, pointed and strong.

1. Oriolus oriolus (Golden Oriole)

The sexes differently coloured. Male is mostly a bright yellow, base wings and tail that are black. The female is olive-green on back and head while underparts are a black-flecked grey. Length 24 cms. A bird of passage but also summer visitor to the forests of both ranges.

Laniidae Family

Medium-sized birds. Tail long, head big; legs slender, bill thick and strong, on the whole short, the upper lip down-curved at corners.

1. Lanius minor (Lesser Grey Shrike)

Grey on back and crown. Underparts very pale greyish-beige. Wings and tail black. A wide black band on eyes. Length 20 cms. A spring bird of passage.

2. Lanius senator (Woodchat Shrike)

Similar to 1 except that the crown of head is brownish-red. Length 17 cms. A summer visitor and passing migrant.

3. Lanius collurio (Red-backed Shrike)

Similar to 1 but wings and back brown. Length 17 cms. A passing migrant. It is probable that some pairs remain on the Troodos Range during summer. Besides the typical form individuals with a brown tail have been observed in Cyprus. They may possibly belong to the subspecies **isabellinus** and **phoenicuroides.**

4. Lanius nubicus (Masked Shrike)

Similar with 1 but back and crown of head black. Length 17 cms. A very common summer visitor to the Cyprus mountains.

Corvidae Family

Either large - or medium - sized birds.Tail either long or medium. Colours either bright or dark. Legs relatively strong. Variety of bills.

1. Corvus Corax (Raven)

Coal-black, strong legs. Thick, strong bill. Length 64 cms. Eats anything. Once a very common resident. Today rather rare, especially in the mountains.

2. Corvus frugilegus (Rook)

Similar to 1 but smaller. 46 cms. Both bill and grey legs more slender. A rare winter visitor.

3. Corvus corone - subsp. cornix (Hooded Crow)

Like 1 but smaller - 47 cms. Bill more slender, belly and back grey. The populations found in Cyprus are considered by many to belong to a separate race of W. Asia (C. c. sardonius). A common permanent resident.

Lesser Grey Shrike

Raven

Hooded Crow

Cyprus Jay

4. Corvus monedula - subsp. soemmerringii (Jackdaw)

Like 1 but much smaller, only 33 cms. long. Slender bill. Back of head light grey (in the typical subspecies it is dark grey). Quite a common permanent resident. In wintertime more birds from farther north come to winter in Cyprus.

5. Pica pica (Magpie)

Tail very long, wedge-shaped at tip and dark olive-green. Head, back, wings, lower belly, throat, and breast black. Belly and base of wings white. Length 46 cms.

6. Garrulus glandarius - subsp glaszneri (Cyprus Jay)

Belly, breast, and head dark beige. Black specks on crown of head, and a black line, like a moustache, on either side of bill. Tail black. Back grey. Throat white. Wings black with one part dark blue and a white spot on it. An endemic Cyprian form. A common permanent resident.

Sturnidae Family

Birds resembling the **corvidae** but smaller. Bill straight and slender.

1. Sturnus vulgaris (Starling)

Almost coal-black in summer, black with white speckles in winter. Legs a greyish red. Bill greyish-yellow. Length 21.5 cms. A very common winter visitor. Flies in large flocks which roost at night in tall trees.

2. Sturnus roseus (Rose-coloured Starling)

Similar to 1 in outline but back and belly pink. Length 21.5 cms. A rare bird of pass-age.

Passeridae Family

Small birds with a short, conical bill. Feed chiefly on seeds.

1. Passer domesticus -subsp. biblicus (House Sparrow)

Top of body a greyish-brown mottled with darker specks. Underparts greyish-white. Breast and throat black. Crown of head grey. The hen sparrow - without black on breast and throat. Length 14.5 cms. A common permanent resident. Lives everywhere - in the forests, in the fields, in the villages and in the towns.

2. Passer hispaniolensis (Spanish Sparrow)

Similar to 1 but in the cock sparrow the crown of head is brown and the black of breast extends in flecks down towards belly. Length 14.5 cms. A common enough permanent resident, especially wherever there are forests.

3. Passer Montanus (Tree Sparrow)

Like 1 and 2 but only the throat is black in the male. There is also a black spot on either side of the head. 14 cms long. A rather rare winter visitor.

4. Passer moabiticus (Dead Sea Sparrow)

Like 1 but darker and smaller (12 cms). Only throat is black. Head grey with two yellow spots on sides. The hen paler than No. 1 hen. An endemic species of the Middle East. Was first observed in Cyprus in 1980. Small populations have established themselves on the island and propagated.

5. Petronia petronia (Rock Sparrow)

Like 1 but cock and hen almost identical with no black on either breast or throat. Crown

Starling

Rose-coloured Starling

House Sparrow

Dead Sea Sparrow

and back of head pale grey. The male has one yellow spot on breast. A rare winter visitor.

Fringilidae Family

Birds very similar to those of previous families. Differences almost imperceptible.

1. Fringilla coelebs (Chaffinch)

Male's breast, belly, throat, and lower part of head brownish. Back of head grey. Tail greyish-black. Wings greyish-black with two characteristic white bars towards base. Female identical in wings and tail, but the rest of body a uniform grey-beige. 15 cms. A permanent Cyprus resident which, however, goes to the highlands in summer.

93

2. Fringilla montifringilla (Brambling)

Like 1 as regards wings and tail. Head and back black. Breast a beigy chestnut. Belly white. Female similar but head and back a greyish chestnut mottled with dark specks. Length 14.5 cms. A rare winter visitor.

3. Serinus serinus (Serin)

Upper parts a yellow-green generally, underparts yellowish. Tail dark olive-green. Except for throat and breast the whole plumage is mottled with dark olive-green specks. Female similarly coloured but colours more faded, 11.5 cms in length. Quite a common permanent resident.

4. Serinus pusillus (Red-fronted Serin)

A darkly mottled grey-brown plumage. Head, throat, and breast black. A red spot on brow. Length 12 cms. A W. Asia bird known in Cyprus only from accidental and occasional visits.

5. Carduelis spinus (Siskin)

In general, olive-green, back darker. Breast, throat, and belly yellowish. Tail and wings blackish. Dark flecks on back and flanks. Black crown. Length 12 cms. A winter visitor.

6. Carduelis chloris (Greenfinch)

Like 5 but bigger (14.5 cms) with no dark flecks. A common permanent resident.

7. Carduelis carduelis (Goldfinch)

Male and female practically the same. Body beige. Tail black. Wings black and yellow. Front of head red, sides white, back and crown of head black. Length 12 cms. A common, permanent resident.

8. Carduelis cannabina (Linnet)

Upper parts brown, lower beige. Head beige. Tail white at base, black at tip. Breast and crown of head reddish. Female without red on breast and head, but more speckled. Length 13.5 cms. A permanent resident.

9. Carduelis flammea (Redpoll)

Like 8 but throat black. Length 13-15 cms. Ocaasional winter visitor.

10. Bucanetes (Rhodopechys) githaginea (Trumpeter Finch)

Like 8 and 9 but bill shorter, red on male, yellow on female. Red specks on male's body. Length 12.5 cms. A rare African visitor.

Chaffinch

Red-fronted Serin

Siskin

Linnet

11. Carpodacus erythrinus (Scarlet Rosefinch or Scarlet Grosbeak)

Back, wings, and tail brownish. Head, breast, throat: red. Belly beige. Female different: dark grey on top, pale underneath. Bill and legs dark. An E. Europe and Asia bird. Has been observed in Cyprus as an accidental visitor.

12. Coccothraustes coccothraustes (Hawfinch)

In colour resembles a **Chaffinch** but is larger (18 cms). Also bill is thicker and stronger. A winter visitor.

13. Loxia curvirostra-subsp. guillemardi (Cypriot Crossbil)

A characteristic bird. Lives on the Troodos Range, and feeds on pine cone seeds. The tips of the bill are curved and bent in opposite directions so that they cross. This characteristic has given it its name. Length 16.5 cms. The female is greenish with a grey crown and back, and wings and tail blackish. The male which in the typical form is reddish in the Cyprian subspecies resembles the female. Reddish individuals appear only rarely. The bill is bigger and stronger than that of the typical form. An endemic subspecies of the widely distributed in Eurasia Loxia curvirostra. A permanent resident in the mountain forests.

Emberizidae Family

Birds almost the same in appearance as those belonging to the **Passeridae** and **Fringilidae** families. They are different in perceptible characteristics and are somewhat bigger in size.

1. Emberiza melanocephala (Black-headed Bunting)

Male yellow beneath and brown above. Wings and tail blackish. Black head. The female has beige underparts, and grey-brown with dark flecks on upper parts. Length 16.5 cms. A summer visitor from Asia where it winters.

2. Emberiza citrinella (Yellowhammer)

Same as 1 but male's head yellowish. Length 16.5 cms. A rare winter visitor.

3. Emberiza caesia (Cretzschmar's Bunting)

Belly beige - brown, back, wings, and tail beige with brownish-black flecks and stripes. Head and breast grey. Throat beige-brown. The female similar but slightly more flecked, and colours duller. Length 16.5 cms. A common summer visitor.

4. Emberiza hortulana (Ortolan Bunting)

Almost the same as 3 but throat yellowish, head and breast grey-olive-green. Length 16.5 cms. Quite a common bird of passage.

5. Emberiza cia (Rock Bunting)

Like 4 but on head there are three black bars on either side. The head is grey, throat and 'eyebrows' almost white. The female grey-brown with dark specks. Length 16 cms.

6. Emberiza leucocephala (Pine Bunting)

Similar to 5 but head brown with crown and 'cheeks' white. Breast with brown specks and a white collar. Belly white. Length 16,5 cm. An Asiatic species observed on the Troodos Range as an accidental visitor.

7. Emberiza schoeniclus (Reed Bunting)

Underparts white, upper brown with dark flecks. Head, throat, and breast black. Two white

Trumpeter Finch

Scarlet Rosefinch

Black-headed Bunting

Cretzschmar's Bunting

lines begin from the bill and form collar round neck. The female grey-brown with dark specks. Length 15 cms. A common winter visitor.

8. Emberiza aureola (Yellow-breasted Bunting)

Like 7 but underparts yellow. A yellow and brown collar encircles throat. An Asia and N. E. Europe species, accidentally and occasionally appearing in Cyprus.

9. Emberiza cineracea (Cinereous Bunting)

Upper parts grey with dark specks, pale grey on underparts. Head grey-olive-green. Length 16.5 cms. Not a very common bird of passage.

10. Miliaria (Emberiza) calandra (Corn Bunting)

Male and female almost identical, grey-brown with dark specks. Length 18 cms. A common resident.

ACCIDENTAL APPEARANCES

There are reports of accidental appearances in earlier or relatively recent years of the following species:

Anser fabalis, Aegolius funereus, Aquila rapax, Ammomanes cincturus, Anthus gustavi, Acrocephalus paludicola, Acrocephalus dumetorum, Branta bernicla, Branta ruficolis, Charadrius mongolus, Caprimulgus aegyptius, Elanus caerulus, Emberiza cirlus, Emberiza pusilla, Falco biarmicus,Gavia stellata, Hoplopterus tectus, Lanius excubitor, Loxia leucoptera, Oenanthe xanthoprymna, Oenanthe lugens, Puffinus gravis, Pterocles exustus, Pycnonotus barbatus, Phylloscopus trochiloides, Parus caerulus, Picus sp. (viridis?), Petronia petronia, Sterna bengalensis, Surnia ulula, Strix aluco, Sitta neumayer.

INTRODUCTIONS

From time to time, since the end of the last century up to recently, different species of birds have been introduced into Cyprus. On the whole these introductions have not been very successful. The introduced species are as follows:

Ammoperdix hegi-1937 (unsuccessfully), Perdix perdix-1883 (unsuccessfully), Phasianus colchicus- 1880, 1910, 1952, 1968, 1971 (unsuccessfully), Streptopelia roseogrisea (risonia)-1963 survived at least up to 1975 and bred in Nicosia. At the present it seems to have disappeared.

Yellow-breasted Bunting

Corn Bunting

Baby sparrows in their nest. Many bird species have adapted marvellously to human urban life.

SEA MAMMALS

Unlike the birds of Cyprus, the sea mammals of the Cyprus waters are not at all well-known and very few studies have been carried out on them. Only scant information is available regarding these species which belong to two groups: the flippered and the cetaceans. From the information we have, we conclude that the following species are encountered in the Cyprus area.

Delphinidae Family

Cetaceans of relatively small or medium size, and a body perfectly adapted to fast swimming. The nose may be long (Dolphins) or short (Porpoises). They have a blow-hole on the nape. They bear and nurse their young in the sea.

1. Tursiops truncatus (Bottle-nosed Dolphin)

The body is like a fish's while the mouth resembles a beak. It has a medium - sized dorsal fin on its back. It is a uniform grey. The greatest length in the older individuals is 3.60 m. It resides in the waters surrounding the island and moves in schools. It feeds on various sea animals. It is less common than the following dolphin.

2. Delphinus delphis (Common Dolphin)

Similar to previous one, but smaller (up to 2.60 m). Grey-black on upper part, and with yellow flanks and a pale belly. There are also two characteristic white bands on flanks. It feeds on fish, cephalopods and other sea animals. It moves in schools in the waters surrounding Cyprus, and is, as yet, quite common.

3. Phocaena phocaena (Common or Harbour Porpoise)

Similar to the two foregoing ones, but smaller, up to 2 m. long, grey-black on upper parts and almost white beneath. Its nose is very short. It lives in schools and feeds on different sea animals.

4. Globicephale melaena (Pilot, or Caa'ing, or Grindhval Whale)

A very big dolphin reaching up to 8.50 m. It is dark grey, its head round, and has no nose. Rare accidental appearances in the Cyprus waters.

5. Grambus griseus (Risso's Dolphin)

A rare Cyprus visitor which looks like a bottle-nosed dolphin but is larger, attaining 4m. in length, and lacks a snout.

6. Orcinus orca (Killer Whale)

This cetacean, too, is an enormous dolphin, reaching up to 9.50 m. It is distinguished by its two-coloured body, black above and white below. The dorsal fin is particularly long, especially in the males. A carnivore, it feeds on dolphins, seals and large fish. It is the

Common Dolphin   Pilot or Caa-ing

Cuvier's Whale

only Mediterranean cetacean that is dangerous to man, though not rarely it can become his best friend. The Killer Whales were plentiful all over the Mediterranean in former times. Today they rarely make an appearance, and naturally they are seldom seen in Cyprus waters.

Physeteridae Family

Medium to large-sized cetaceans with big heads. They bear and nurse their young in the sea.

1. Ziphus cavirostris (Cuvier's Whale)

A grey, long-nosed catecean. Up to 8 m. in length. A rare accidental visitor to the seas around Cyprus.

101

Phocidae Family

Limbs converted into flippers with an elongated body, tapering towards tail and ending in two flukes. Earless with only two orifices that occlude when in the water. The front and hind flippers are identical. In these flippers one can discern the digital skeleton while claws protrude from the tips. Their teeth are like those of carnivores. They are harmless to man.

Monachus monachus (Monk Seal)

This is the sole flippered mammal to be found in Cyprus. Its skin is covered with thick, short silky fur, dark brown above and paler on the underparts. In the bulls one part of the belly is white. This seal can reach a length of 2.70 m., and 320 kgs. in weight. One pup. Dwells in sea-caves whose entrances are usually below the surface of the sea. In Cyprus the Mediterranean seal is to be found in the region of the Akamas Peninsula. An endangered species protected by international and Cyprian legislation.

LAND AND FLYING MAMMALS

As unknown as the sea mammals, perhaps even more so, are the land mammals. While there is some information about certain medium and large-sized species, for others, and in particular where small mammals such as Bats and Rodents are concerned, the forthcoming information is extremely meagre and confused.

Below follow the descriptions of species that certainly must exist in Cyprus. This, of course, does not preclude the existence of other species as well. In fact, certain species not mentioned are bound, because of their cosmopolitan range, to be found on Cyprus too.

Bovidae Family

Herbivore ruminants of medium or large size, with cloven hooves. On their heads there are usually, permanent, hollow horns that grow longer with age. In the males they are as a rule larger.

1. Ovis musimon - subsp. orientalis (Cyprian or Red Sheep)

This animal resembles the domestic sheep in size and general outline, but its hairy coat is very much shorter. The male attains a length of about 1.20 m., while the female is smaller. The winter coat is thick, relatively long, and light brown in colour. Towards the back and flanks it gets paler in the males, especially in older animals. The adult males have a mane extending from throat to chest. In females the colour is more uniform. In summer the coat is short and lighter in colour and white on the belly. The female's horns are very short, whereas those of the males are large, thick and curved. The older the animal the more curved its horns.

Mating takes place in the autumn, the males butting each other fiercely and noisily to win the female. In spring the females bear one lamb, in rare cases two.

Monk Seal

Cyprian or Red Sheep

The Cyprian Wild Sheep is endemic to the island, that is to say it exists in no other part of the world. Formerly it was considered a separate species or a subspecies of the Asiatic ammon. But the prevailing opinion today is that it is a subspecies of the Musimon (Mouflon) which lives in Sardinia and Corsica, and has been introduced into several European countries. Various other subspecies of the Musimon live in Asia, from Turkey to Mongolia, while up to the 15th century there were wild mountain sheep in Crete as well. In the past, the Cyprus Wild Sheep lived on all the mountain ranges of Cyprus. Between 1920 and 1930 its spread was limited solely to the Paphos forests and to Mount Olymbos (Hionistra) of the Troodos Range. By 1937 there remained only a small flock of about 15 animals. It is since then that the legislation for the protection of the Cyprian Wild Sheep and the strict supervision of the whole area have come into force. At present, the Wild Sheep live in the Paphos forest on West Troodos and number over a thousand individuals, thus appearing to have escaped the danger of extinction.

Canidae Family

Carnivores, more or less dog-like in their general characteristics. They are terrestrial, capable of putting on speed when hunting their prey; unable to climb. Their teeth are the typical teeth of carnivores with highly developed canines.

1. Vulpes vulpes (Fox)

Rather like a small-sized dog but distinguishable by its sharp pointed muzzle and long bushy tail. Body length up to 60 cms. brush up to 40 cms. The colour varies according to habitat, usually though it is a light chestnut, except for the tail tip and the belly that are white. Lives in forests and the scrub. Its food is birds, rodents and other small animals.

Leporidae Family

Short-tailed herbivores, with big ears and long hind legs which help them run in big bounds. They dig their forms in the ground.

1. Lepus capensis (europaeus) (Brown Hare)

Like a rabbit but larger up to 55 cm. in length and 3 kg. in weight, and ears and hind legs longer. 3-4 litters a year, each consisting of 2-4 leverets, which, in contrast with the young of rabbits born almost naked, are born with a short coat of fur, and eyes open. Greyish in colour, with paler belly; usually have a white spot on forehead. Ubiquitous. Feeds on plants.

Erinaceidae Family

Terrestrial animals. Their coat has spine hair as well as coarse hair, especially on upper part of body.

Fox

Browr Hare (juvenile)

Oriental Hedgehog

Ship Rat

1. Hemiechinus auritus (Oriental Hedgehog)

A small animal of the insectivore order, 18-25 cm. in length. Its body is covered in grey hair and strong spines which can reach 20 cm. Densest and longest on back. The face and limbs are a greyish-black. It is to be found almost everywhere from the coast up to the mountain zone, in fields, scrub and glades. It eats insects, snails, fruit, frogs and even dead animals. Pesticides play havoc with the hedgehogs.

Muridae Family

Rodents with either a short or long hairless tail. Mainly nocturnal.

1. Rattus rattus-subsp. frugivorus (Ship Rat)

A large nocturnal rodent dwelling in basements, storehouses, sewers, etc. A long hairless tail. Dark grey, belly white. Length of body 16.5-22.8 cm. Length of tail up to 25 cms. Ubiquitous. Five litters a year, 5-10 in a litter. Omnivorous. The species was introduced into Europe in the Middle Ages from Asia.

2. Mus musculus (House Mouse)

A small global mouse. Body length: 7-9 cms. Tail about the same length. Fur grey or greyish-brown, belly paler. 10 litters a year. 5-6 in a litter. Omnivorous, but especially partial to grains. Cosmopolitans. Found in human habitations and fields.

3. Acomys nesiotes (Cyprian Spiny Mouse)

A rare species. Stiff bristles on back, otherwise like a common mouse. Greyish-brown, belly lighter-coloured. Body length: 9-11 cms. tail slightly longer. 1-5 in a litter, born with eyes open. Found in rocky, dry localities. Feeds mainly on grains, but will eat anything it finds. Endemic to Cyprus.

Rhinolophidae Family

Includes small-sized bats with a fleshy protuberance above nose, whence the name of the family. Ears pointed.

1. Rhinolophus hipposideros (Lesser Horseshoe Bat)

Length, including tail, 9 cms. Wingspan about 22 cms. Greyish-beige, wing membranes darker, blackish. Sporadic appearances. Hibernation in caves, hanging by feet.

2. Rhinolophus blasii (Blasius's Horsehoe Bat)

Identical with 1 but body beige and wings light chestnut.

Vespertilionidae Family

A relatively small bat; head resembling a mouse's, without a fleshy protuberance over nose.

1. Eptesicus serotinus (Serotine Bat)

Distinguished by its dark grey colour, and rounded ears. Quite a common species.

2. Miniopterus schreibersii (Schreiber's Bat)

Similar to 1 but snout very short, colour light grey.

3. Myotis blythi (Lesser mouse-eared Bat)

Distinguished by its pale chestnut colour, and its big ears.

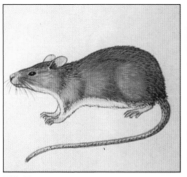

Ship Rat

House Mouse

Blasius's Horseshoe Bat

Serotine Bat

Family Pteropidae

Relatively large bats with big, round eyes. Feed on fruit.

1. Rusettus aegyptiacus (Egyptian Fruit Bat)

A rare North Africa and West Asia species. A large, dark-grey bat. Hibernates in caves. In summer lives on fruit, largely on figs. Its head reminds one of the lemurs of Madagascar.

Soricidae Family

Insectivore animals, in outline like mice, but with a very long pointed muzzle.

Schreiber's Bat

Egyptian Fruit Bat

1. Crocidura cypria (Cyprus Pygmy Shrew)

Greyish-beige animals, belly paler. Length of body without tail about 5 cms long. Nocturnal habits.

Acknowledgements

I wish to express my warm thanks to Messrs. A. Demetropoulos, C. Tsimilis, P. Neophytou, L. Pinghouras, Teucros Constantinou, G. Mavroudis and all the other good friends of the Pancyprian Ecological Movement, for their unstinted help and support. Similarly to the Authorities of the Ministry of Agriculture and Natural Resources for the information and maps they gave me.

A landscape of the Akamas Peninsula which is one of the most important habitats of Cyprus fauna.

A now of the peninsula of Akama. The open fields, the heath and the small and large ravines in the area serve as an ideal habitat for the birds of prey.

A view in the western section of the Troodos Range. We can discern two endemic plants of Cyprus: Cedrus libanii-brevifolia, and Quercus alnifolia.

BIRDS INDEX OF LATIN NAMES

BIRDS
INDEX OF ENGLISH NAMES

INDEX OF MAMMALS
SCIENTIFIC NAMES

INDEX OF MAMMALS
COMMON ENGLISH NAMES

BIBLIOGRAPHY

Attenborough D.: «The First Eden - The Mediterranean World and Man» London 1987

Fint P.R. & Stewart P.F.: «The Birdds of Cyprus» London 1983

Heinzel H. - Fitter R. & Parslow J.: «The Birds of Britain and Europe, with N. Africa and the Middle East» London 1972

Hill G.: «The History of Cyprus»

Khristis Glafkos: «Agrino. To spanio Agrioprovato tis Kyprou» Magazine «Gyneka» (Woman)

Kharalampidis C. - Kharalampidis M. - Neophytou P.: «The Birds of Cyprus» Nicosia 1985

Meikle R.D.: «Flora of Cyprus» Vol. 1 Kew 1977

Meikle R.D.: «Flora of Cyprus» Vol. 2

Mallison J.: «The Shadow of Extinction - Europe's Threatenend Wild Mammals» London 1978

Osorio - Tafall B.F. & Serafim G.M.: «List of the Vascular Plants of Cyprus»

Panayotou A.: «Geology» Great Cypriot Encyclopedia

Further Comments

Cyprus State Forests Map - Department of Lands and Surveys Cyprus 1984

Geological Map of Cyprus - Geological Survey Department, Cyprus 1979.

The illustrations

The illustrations in this book have been made possible due to a combination of a large number of methods. Many of the photographs come from slides belonging to my good friends Triandafyllos Adamacopoulos, and Gregory Tsounis, both of whom I warmly thank for their valuable assistance. There are also slides of my own.

In the case of many rare species, it was difficult to find any photographs so I have used paintings of these species, which are faithful reproductions I had painted with the intention of publishing an album. Before using these paintings here I had to make slides of them.

For some species I have used the montage method superimposing the bird or mammal on the suitable background so that the result resembles an actual photograph.

Unfortunately to illustrate the whole book using slides or paintings is a difficult, expensive and time-consuming affair. However, I hope that it will be possible in the future to publish a larger-sized book with paintings of all the birds and mammals of Cyprus.

G. Sfikas.

CONTENTS